Self-Discipline Science

&

Daily Self-Discipline

-2 In 1-

The Hidden Truth That Keeps You Procrastinating And How To Stop It

By

Valentine Downey

Table of Contents

Self-Discipline Science

Daily Self-Discipline

Self-Discipline Science

How To Make Self-Discipline Feel
Completely Natural

By

Valentine Downey

Introduction

If you lack self-discipline, then you can see the trickledown effects in every part of your life. You have low self-esteem, poor time management, and low success rates in the ventures you undertake. From procrastination to ill health, a lack of self-discipline infects every part of your life.

Sound familiar? Then you have picked up the right book.

After a decade of studying and research self-discipline, I am here to provide you with real, science-based facts about how to develop yourself into a successful person. This is not like any other self-improvement book; it isn't some motivational poster expanded into a book full of blah-blah-blah. It is a proven approach that will give you results.

Once you have finished this book, you will know the secret formula to making yourself invincible in all endeavors. You will know how to take care of yourself, attack work with vigor, and attract success like a magnet. You will find out how to follow things through to the very end, from diets to entrepreneurial endeavors. Self-discipline will help you achieve success in all areas of life and allow you to become the person you have always wanted to be.

During my ten-year tenure working as a consultant for business owners and entrepreneurs, I have helped many people achieve success that they never thought possible. The most notable achievement I saw was a lady who weighed three hundred and fourteen pounds when she came to see me. She wanted some help learning how to run her own business, but my advice helped her become a successful entrepreneur *and* lose weight. This is because I taught her the secret of science-based self-discipline. Now I want to teach these things to you. I love helping others and I have found that self-discipline is the only skill I need to teach you so that you can help yourself.

I promise that from this day forward, you will be a better person. You will no longer feel like a failure or wish that you had control. You will no longer engage in bad habits and put your health, sanity, and success at risk. Finally, you will actually start to like yourself and feel proud of your life. This book will revolutionize your life, transforming it from the ground up.

Stop putting things off, stop letting your dreams slip away, and stop failing yourself. The longer you wait to develop self-discipline, the more your life will spiral out of control. You need to take control today by reading this book and getting real results in your life.

So don't wait any longer. Learn the secret formula to success that lies in developing self-discipline. Based on real science, these methods are tried and true. You will see the change you want within days of reading of this book and taking action.

Chapter 1: The Biological Basis of Self-Discipline

Why do some people have lots of self-discipline, and others don't? You see the disciplined ones running at 5 am and finishing projects well before the deadline. Then you see the non-disciplined ones, who can't stop eating after they are full and who procrastinate to the point of ruin. There is a biological reason behind why some people possess this highly desirable trait and others don't. This hardly means that you can't change your DNA, however, as you will see later.

Is There a Biological Basis for Personality?

A popular belief is that people fit into either the Type A category or the Type B category. Type A's are perfectionists to the point of neurosis, display hostility, and are fiercely competitive, whereas Type B's are more relaxed. This theory started in 1976, when cardiologist Friedman and Rosenman noticed that their cardiac patients were particularly nervous, agitated, and energetic, to the point that they wore through the upholstery in the waiting room chairs.[1] The personality traits of Type A people tended to cause high stress, which caused hypertension and other issues. This was why the patients of Friedman and Rosenman suffered higher rates of cardiac problems compared to other, more relaxed people.[1]

The truth is that there may be some scientific basis to this difference, but overall it is a myth. Personality falls upon a continuum, where people have varying levels of certain traits like competitiveness, hostility, and internal or external motivation. People all react to stressful events differently, and also anticipate events differently, which results in the observed Type A/Type B differences and overall effects on health.[1] But there is no set way to label one's personality, and personality can vary or change with events, circumstances, and age.

Whether personality is caused by nature or nurture is a subject of hot debate in the science community. Twin studies help prove that two people with the same genetics can still turn out differently, pointing toward environment and life experience as a major factor in personality development. And yet, twins who are separated at birth will grow up with striking similarities, pointing toward a more genetic basis for personality.[2] Jim Springer and Jim Lewis were separated at just four weeks of age, yet grew up to be identical – they smoked the same cigarettes, drove the same car, went to the same beach in Florida, and bit their nails.[2] Obviously genetics play some huge role in how your personality turns out.

A study on psychotic serial killers has also helped researchers make great strides in the nature vs. nurture debate as well. The findings of these studies have pinpointed that psychopaths in particular have abnormal brain structures in the "social areas" of the brain, mainly the anterior rostral prefrontal cortex and temporal poles. Whether these abnormalities are caused by environmental factors or genetics is debatable, but obviously gray matter has a tremendous impact on personality. So your personality is indeed related to the shape of your brain…but why it forms is still unknown.[3]

The most common and logical consensus is that you have a set personality created by your genes. Robert M. Glatter from Lenox Hill Hospital in Northwell Health explains the process: How you are raised either changes or reinforces your temperament.[4] As time passes, people will respond to you certain ways based on your temperament, thus hammering it down into your development. By adulthood, you have developed your personality based on upbringing, genetics, and life events and it's pretty set in stone, at least to your mind.[5]

The nature vs. nurture debate is not terribly important in the long run. How we got where we are today is irrelevant when you consider that you can change yourself. But it is useful to know that your personality is predetermined, at least partially, by genetics. This piece of knowledge can make you worry that your inability to develop self-discipline is going to be permanently impossible simply because it's written into your genes. But science proves that you not use that as an excuse.

few tries at it, the brain stops working so hard and starts to treat the new skill as an automatic process.[7]

The only explanation for this is that the brain creates new networks to make the processes necessary for each skill faster and more efficient. This proves that as you practice something, it rewires your brain. Think back to how much you struggled when you were first learning to write. Now you do it without thinking about it. See how your brain formed a new network of neurons to let you write?

What is even more fascinating about this research is that this response is universal. Everyone's brains respond the same way to newly learned skills.[7] This means that anyone, including you, can learn the skill of self-discipline and restructure your brain to make it an automatic, effortless facet of your personality.

Chapter 2: The Reasons People Have Developed Self-Discipline

Studying those with self-discipline can help you develop your own self-discipline. This is because the human brain is hardwired to look up to models to form its own patterns. The tendency to do this stems from childhood, when we look up to our parents for models on how to behave.[35] The brain makes adaptations to itself based on early models, which in turn affects how it grows.[35]

The best role models for self-discipline are successful entrepreneurs. Looking into their behavior and daily routines will give you some insight into how to structure your own life and behavior. When you see that other people do things, it makes you more motivated to do it yourself, as a study regarding tax collection letters in Britain has found.[10] Previously these letters were ineffective, but after adding the sentence "Other people are paying their taxes," tax debt has shot down £3.5 billion.

Why Have People Developed Self-Discipline?

It is true that some people are born with a healthy level of self-discipline in their personalities. They are naturals at being efficient and hardworking. Usually this stems from how they were raised as well as possible genetic elements.

However, these people are not any different from you. They just happen to have developed a skill that you have not developed yet. Through hard work and dedication, they have taught themselves how to manage their time and motivate themselves to go after long-term rewards. They have also learned how to manage and tolerate discomfort, which we cover in a later chapter.

It is not true that self-discipline starts in childhood. Your parents can teach you good habits, but you are exposed to a wealth of other influences that can alter your behavior as you grow older. In fact, it has been found that children learn more from their peers than their parents, according to research by notable independent researcher Judith Harris.[8] A rigid, structured childhood does not necessarily make you behave that way as an adult.

However, influences later in life can form the lasting habits that self-disciplined people use. Many self-disciplined people come from military backgrounds, where they were trained to be extremely disciplined and neat. Others learned by emulating role models, such as self-disciplined peers or sports coaches. Yet others taught themselves through books and practice.

No matter your background, you can learn self-discipline too. The best way is by finding out why you lack self-discipline, covered in the next chapter, and then start making small lifestyle changes that bring more discipline and structure into your daily life.

Learning to Believe in Yourself

One thing you will notice that is common between most self-disciplined people is their commitment to getting up early, meditating for at least a few minutes, and eating nutritious foods. By starting with small lifestyle changes, they developed a sort of discipline that spilled into other areas of their lives.[9] Small steps toward self-discipline appear to work quite well in changing your brain's overall performance and attitude.

Why is this?

Harry Truman made a great statement that summarizes this sentiment: "In reading the lives of great men, I found that the first victory they won was over themselves... self-discipline with all of them came first."[9]

When you take small actions, you are essentially winning a war with yourself. You are proving to your brain that you can do this. As your brain accepts this truth, it starts to actually believe it. Many studies have found that when your brain believes something, it sticks to it with dogged determination.[11]

In your past, this could spell very bad news. If you believed, "I can't do this self-discipline thing because I'm just not a disciplined person," then your brain wholeheartedly didn't even try because it bought into this negative core belief. But now, if you believe that you can do it, then your brain will give it all its got. Your thoughts about yourself are self-fulfilling prophecies.[11]

However, you can't just believe something without proof, right? You need to prove it to yourself. This is why taking baby steps can revolutionize your entire life. Prove to yourself that you can be self-disciplined with small actions and see that disciplined action spill into all other areas of your life. At this point, your brain will start to apply what it has started to believe to everything, bringing about attitude adjustment and subsequent personality change.

Learn these traits of self-disciplined people and then you can start to work on them yourself. In Chapter 4, you will learn even more tips. Step by step, bit by bit, you can build your self-discipline by first proving to yourself that you can. One disciplined action is enough to make you like the very successful and disciplined people in the next section. It all starts with one first step, however, which you can make at any time to begin training your brain.

Universal Traits of Self-Disciplined People and Why They Work

No matter who your role model is, here are some crucial traits that are practically universal to highly successful and self-disciplined people. In Chapter 4, you learn more about each of these traits and how to develop them within yourself.

Routine. Mark Zuckerburg is quoted telling an audience, "I really want to clear my life to make it so that I have to make as few decisions as possible about anything except how to best serve this community."[13] This is why he follows the same daily routine, eats "whatever" for breakfast, and wears the same exact outfit every day.

Routine makes efficiency quite possible. When you have a routine, your brain knows exactly what to do next because it is always the same. Thus, you eliminate the amount of decisions you make throughout the course of your day.

This creates efficiency. Movements in the body create change in the environment, which the brain must process. If the brain has already processed this change in the past, however, it must expend less work. As a result, the brain prefers habits, which create less work for it to do.[14] Routine makes discipline easier on the brain, so that it is more possible and one can devote more time to other tasks.

Continued Education. Highly self-disciplined people don't just stay content with what they learned in school. They continue to stay current in their fields by subscribing to relevant periodicals with industry news, attending seminars, and taking classes. Some careers even require continuing education classes.

Imagine a doctor who doesn't stay up-to-date with advances in medicine. As new and better medical technology is developed, he would refuse to use it, thus holding his staff and patients back from improvements in health. As certain theories are disproved, he would never know, thus endangering his patients with unsafe and unhelpful treatments.

To stay useful and relevant in the world, you must update your knowledge on topics and never stop learning. It is the best way to stay useful in your field of work.

In addition, learning is a good way to develop more intelligence. Learning triggers more neural growth, we learned already.[7] You can trigger more brain growth and more smarts by learning new skills. You will never be old to learn.

Reading. Bill Gates tries to complete one book a week. He is an example of how absorbing more information in the Information

Age is essential. Reading in one's industry (and about other industries as well) helps one stay relevant and expand one's conscious awareness of the world.[15]

Reading plays in with the previous trait of continuing education, but it also has unique benefits of its own. It enables one to form new connections within the brain and find new ways of looking at the world, allowing one to formulate creative solutions to problems.[15] It enhances education, creativity, and critical thinking all at once, making it a powerful tool for growing diversity and intelligence.[15] Reading diverse things that don't relate to your industry increase the odds of you make creative connections.

Imagine that you have encountered a new problem with a merger at work. Everyone in your company is totally stumped. But you happen to be reading Russian novels at the time and you draw some inspiration about diplomacy from political scenes in *War and Peace.* You just made a connection no one else could because of what you read, and thus you found the solution that no one else found.

Meditating. Meditation is not just a New Age hocus pocus time waster. It is actually effective for training and honing the mind, leading to greater mental mastery and self-control.[16] Strong believers in the power of meditation include Ariana Huffington (journalist and Huffington Post CEO), Jeff Weiner (former Yahoo! CEO), and Jerry Seinfeld (actor and comedian).

Meditation has been found to decrease depression, anxiety, chronic pain, and aging.[16] Part of this is because focused mindfulness meditation has actually been found to reduce activity in the default mode network, aka "monkey mind center" of the brain, in MRIs performed by Yale University. Activity in this part of the brain has been linked to scattered thoughts, which are common causes of distracted thinking that lead to reduced productivity and concentration, intrusive thoughts that lead to depression, and even insomnia that is triggered by too much thinking activity.[16]

John Hopkins University studies have also found that meditation allows for enough mental control to ease mental illness and pain.[16] A person who practices regular meditation can gain enough self-control to regulate and redirect thoughts and block out physical sensations.

Meditation also gives time for reflection on the day's activities. This allows people to review what they want to accomplish in the day ahead and how they could have done better in the day previous.[17] Doing this can allow you to grow as a person and decide what actions to take to become more successful, which goes hand in hand with self-discipline.

Treating their bodies as temples. Craig Esreal was an obese child, but he's turned that around now.[19] From taking the stairs to providing yoga classes to his managers to only serving healthy food in his company, he shows that healthy CEOs are more successful.[19]

Self-discipline involves adopting healthy habits that increase your body's resiliency. A view many self-disciplined people adopt, either consciously or subconsciously, is that their bodies are sacred temples that must treated as such. This view prevents these people from doing anything that violates their temples, such as eating poorly or smoking.

When you are in tiptop shape, it follows that you are able to function better mentally. In-shape CEOs also make a better impression and thus garner more respect and better treatment.[19] You can, too.

Exercising. Warren Buffet exercises every day. Mark Zuckerburg exercises three times a week by running with his dog. Obama makes sure to shoot hoops for 45 minutes a day and run three miles six days a week.[18]

These self-disciplined people didn't always like exercise. Buffett had to start exercising at a recommendation from his doctors, and Obama used to engage in casual drug use and other unhealthy habits.[18] But all of these people include exercise in their routines anyway because they know that health is the priority.[18] They tolerate discomfort and dread of exercise in order to take care of themselves and push on for greater success.

Exercise also creates an energy rush, or a natural high, which can help you balance hormones to manage moods and stress well and which can help you stay more motivated throughout the day.[20] It lowers your risk of diseases, increase your self-esteem as you look better, and improves immunity and memory so that you miss out on less.[20] If you want to be at your best, exercise is the way to go.

Waking up early. Most CEOs that you read about wake up early, giving them to eat, exercise, work out, and meditate before the workday officially starts. This habit allows them regular sleep schedules and more time in the day to get things done before others do. This is why it can appear that self-disciplined people have more time in the day than the average non-disciplined person.

The human brain operates on a Circadian rhythm, where its performance is influenced by what time it is. For some reason, it operates best when you wake up early because it feels that it has more time to get things done.[21] Waking up early lets you achieve more in the day, have more energy, and accomplish things like exercise well before you are expected to show up to work.

There are also unexpected health benefits. One thing early rising does is make you regulate your sleep cycle along your natural Circadian rhythm.[21] That way you get healthy sleep, which lowers the risk of obesity and improves your immune system.[21] The *Journal of Psychiatric Research* draws from a new study that indicates better sleep equals less mental illness and high productivity.[21]

Saying no. A self-disciplined person can say no to that chocolate donut. He can say no to taking on too much work. He can say no to people who are demanding too much of him.

Saying no is more powerful than you think. You look at something and measure the cost versus benefit. If the costs are too great to be worth the benefit, then you politely decline.[17] Setting boundaries through this cost-benefit analysis enables you to focus on what is actually important and what can be turned down.[17]

For example, the chocolate donut costs way more calories than you can afford to eat, without giving you any benefit except a second of delight. You also know you will suffer days of regret and guilt. The new project you turn down will take up so much time and energy that you can't give the proper amount to projects you are already working on. And the people who demand too much of you aren't giving you anything except a headache and an ulcer, so you know to say no to them and focus on more rewarding things or people.

Staying Organized. Before work each day, Patrick Gelsinger, CEO of VMWare, organizes his desk and straightens his papers. He color codes his calendar and has his intern tally his time versus his estimates to see how his time management really measures up.[18]

Staying organized gives you more time to focus on what really matters.[17] Having a neat workspace allows for greater concentration because clutter acts as a distraction for your brain. Plus, you are able to dedicate more time to your tasks instead of looking for things lost in the mess.[17]

Having fun. Above, you read about how Warren Buffett exercises religiously. But do you know why he does that? So that he can drink Coke and eat burgers without gaining weight and hurting his health.[18]

Phil Libin, CEO of Evernote, used to work on airplanes. Now he's stopped that and instead kicks back and enjoys the view or conversation and chats on the phone with friends and family.[22]

This goes to show that self-discipline does not have to be about deprivation. Instead, find ways to enjoy yourself and have fun without sabotaging your goals. Seek solutions and workarounds rather than cutting out what you love the most.[23] Brain research has proved that when fun stops, so does learning and work ethic, proving that fun is necessary for your success.[23] You must find a way to have fun and enjoy yourself if you want to be successful. Depriving yourself is not the way to go about this!

Having fun is actually essential to being healthy.[24] So is having some friends and a good social life. Humans are naturally social animals and need to let loose and have a good time with others to stay healthy and sane. A play theorist named Bob Hughes states that play allows us to structure real-life skills and grow as people.[24] In other words, play teaches your mind how to work in real-life scenarios. It is also essential for the release of dopamine and thus stress relief.

Forgiving themselves. Amy Dugan had always been overweight. She had terrible self-discipline when she would slip up and overeat to deal with emotional stress. But after she lost 104 pounds, she is proof that forgiving yourself lessens stress and results in more self-discipline in the long run.[25]

A study discovered that four out of five dieters beat themselves up for slipping up or cheating with food.[25] Meanwhile, almost everyone does slip up – 98% does, actually.[25] Out of this 98%, 78% will never go on to be successful at dieting.[25] This is because they beat themselves for being failures and then drowned their stress and anger in more food. They tended to have the attitude "I already failed, so why not fail worse and eat this whole bag of cookies?"[25] The other 20% who were successful learned to accept cheat meals and even embrace them, thus taking it easier on themselves.

Chapter 3: Find Out Why You Don't Have Self-Discipline

You read about people who do have self-discipline and their excellent habits. While it is great to start emulating these habits today, it is not so easy if self-discipline is a challenge for you. Unearthing the cause of your bad habits and poor self-discipline is a way to start to improve yourself. View it like a disease: You can't treat it if you don't know what's wrong!

There are various bad habits that people with poor self-discipline develop. We will cover each of these individually so you can find what specifically plagues you. Then you can start the journey of self-work and recovery.

Why Do You Procrastinate?

The human brain is an amazing and advanced evolutionary machine. It can process a billion thoughts in a day. It can handle sensory overload and control your bodily functions all at once.

But it is notoriously lazy. Actually, let's edit that statement. Your brain is not lazy per se, but it has such a huge workload that it loves to automate things for efficiency. It loves to do things that guarantee quick rewards and save it effort. Usually, this efficiency is a good thing.

More often than not, your brain won't bother to think things through all of the way. Rather, it relies on automatic representations of the world, or schemas, that you have formed over the course of your lifetime.[26] Your schemas are not always brought about by your personality – they arise from your habits and the things you have been taught or told by your models.[26] They provide fast tracks for your brain to direct your thinking with minimal effort. The issue here is that if you have a negative schema, then you can become stuck in a rut where you repeat unhelpful behaviors.

Procrastination is one example of when this becomes a problem. Procrastination happens when your brain does not see an immediate reward, and instead focuses on other issues based on your schemas. It decides to dread the task and put it off until it's too late. Then you must do a rush job, while stressing yourself out to the max.

If you procrastinate, then you are well aware of how problematic procrastination is. The good news is that procrastination is easily remedied by avoiding mental fatigue and focusing on sources of motivation. You just need to realize what subconscious processes lie behind the procrastination and tackle them.

Here are some of the main causes of procrastination and what you can do about them.

Fear of Failure

Contrary to popular belief, procrastination is seldom caused by laziness. The most common cause of procrastination is a subconscious (meaning you may not be aware of it) fear that you will fail.[27] If you fear failure, then it is far easier and more comfortable to avoid trying altogether.

A good way to overcome this is by focusing on how you might succeed. Think back to your past successes and your qualifications. Think about the end result, if things go the way you want. This can provide some motivation to overcome this fear of failure.

Impulsiveness

Some people struggle with impulse control. Just like when you can't stop yourself from eating something delicious that is placed before you, or you can't say no when your friends dare you to do something outrageous, you also can't stop yourself from following new tasks or distractions.[27]

While you work on one task, you may become tempted to leap onto others that catch your attention. The result is that you become scattered and unable to follow through on any one task. This can lead to procrastination, as you spread yourself too thin and lose interest in your original task.

Break things into priorities and write them down. The thing that takes priority may be the project or task that will take the most time, and have the most significant consequences or results. Focus on that first.

Also, break your tasks into bite-sized chunks that you can accomplish each day. Your brain thinks, "I can do this!" and stays on track. This allows you to accomplish other things by working on other tasks throughout the day as well. You make progress without spreading yourself too thin, and without getting bored.

Rebellion

Humans tend to value personal freedom and free will quite highly.[27] Thus, when you are forced to do something, your first instinct is to rebel by not doing it. Our tendency to do this comes from our instinctual need to be our own persons and to establish dominance over others.

Unfortunately, you can't always say no and be dominant. Your boss is one person who has dominance simply because he or she pays your bills. So when you are told to do a task, you should probably do it.

Thinking of what you can gain can help you overcome your need to rebel. Think about the return – the money, the potential promotion, the way you'll feel. Creating a vision board to make your perceived gains more visual for yourself is a good idea. This is the reason why people like using motivational posters at work.

You might also consider blowing off some steam by focusing on the humor in the situation. Imagine your boss as a cartoon character with a funny voice, get a good laugh in, and then move on. This cathartic release can make your job easier because you indulged your emotions for a bit.

Obsessing over the Unpleasantness

The longer you dwell on how unpleasant or hard something will be, the less you motivate your brain to want to undertake the actions.[27] You create a habit of thinking of tasks as daunting and horrible, which only makes future tasks harder. In this case, your brain's laziness is at work!

You really want to avoid thinking of the negative. Instead, focus on the positive to teach your brain to think of rewards and gains.

Consider how you will benefit and how you will enjoy the work despite its unpleasantness.

Also think of how to make things pleasanter. An example might be streamlining your work system, so that it becomes faster and easier. Another idea is to treat yourself to takeout as you work, so you have yummy food to look forward to and you don't need to cook after working extremely hard. Both of these things count as major rewards to your brain.

Why Do You Allow Distractions?

"Ooh shiny" is the second biggest cause of poor self-discipline. As you let yourself follow any little distraction, you prevent yourself from devoting your full attention and effort on things you need to accomplish. You also mess up your time management with unplanned tasks and prevent yourself from getting things done by the deadline.

Social Distractions

The main distractions people face are social. Human beings are social animals. You are heading to the store but your neighbor wants to chat. You are trying to work but your friend keeps texting about a party this weekend. You are trying to work out but the guy on the treadmill next to you wants to flirt.

All of these things tend to take priority because we enjoy social interaction and we fear being rude and pushing away others. We also get a little dopamine rush, which feels quite good, when we interact with other people positively.[28] James H Fowler and Nicholas Christakis studied over 20,000 people and found that their happiness is contagious up to three degrees of connection.[28] So of course your brain is going to seek out social interaction and let that take precedence over all else. Your brain likes being happy.

A key tip is to minimize social distractions. Put your phone on silent and leave it face down on your desk. Use vacation messages to let people know you will respond to them later. Only check texts and emails at certain times during the day. Prioritize the people you do speak to based on the task at hand. Politely tell people that you are busy and set up another time to chat when you have more free time.

Disorganization

Disorganization in this context can refer to a messy office or home. The brain has too many things to look at and you waste time searching for things. A study suggests that being disorganized and living in chaos takes its toll on your mental functions by causing stress to your brain through sensory overload.[29]

Disorganization can also refer to your time management. Later we talk more about routines and habits, which are important for time management. For the time being, however, understand that not organizing your time properly and assigning specific times to specific things is essential for good time management. It helps you get organized and stay on track with tasks. Not doing so can cause your brain to become overly stressed as well.[29]

Clearly being disorganized is bad and causes your brain to work twice as hard. Getting organized and minimizing clutter can get rid of this problem. Learn to manage your time, your space, and your things. I always recommend a trip to the container store and a daily planner.

Deadlines also help minimize distractions by giving you a time frame to get things organized and in line for work. They also give your brain a more concrete goal to work toward, which seems more real and more achievable. You know what you are working on, so you realize when you don't have time for distractions. Spend the first day getting organized and then the rest working on the task bit by bit.

Multitasking

Western culture values those who get things done. Therefore, many people feel the need to multitask to increase their efficiency and output. Multitasking becomes a habit that bleeds into all areas of life.

Sadly, it's a horrible habit. The reason why is because multitasking reduces the quality with which you focus on things and it makes you less present. One Oxford study found that students who multitask have limited material retention and perform more poorly on tests.[30] They were unable to truly focus and thus commit things to memory.

The lesson here is to stop multitasking. Divide your day into a series of tasks instead. Focus on one thing at a time for better attention, effort, and ultimately memory retention. Your performance will actually shoot up as you stop trying to accomplish too much at once.

Feeling Overwhelmed

When your brain sees a huge project, it senses a massive amount of work. Without a clear starting point, you get confused and overwhelmed. Being overwhelmed is a huge reason why people get distracted, because they are subconsciously trying to focus on other things besides the daunting task at hand. It is your brain's own not-so-brilliant self-sabotage attempt.

Like you read before, bite-sized and ordered chunks of tasks work well for your brain. When you create a to-do list with ordered pieces of each long-term task, your brain actually falls in love.[31] You tend to remember things you need to do better than what you have already done, a phenomena called the Zergarnik effect.[31] First observed by Russian psychologist Bluma Zeigarnik in waiters who forgot what diners ordered right after delivering the meals, it shows that the brain becomes obsessed and anxious about what it must do.[31] To-do lists soothe the brain because you feel as if you are already taking action when you write the list, and you also are less likely to forget, freeing your brain from the stress.[31]

Another idea is to stop viewing the length of time something will take to avoid overwhelming yourself. Addicts in 12-step programs are encouraged to take each day at a time, which shows how the brain does better with small steps instead of looking at a task or a resolution in its totality. So if you are on a diet, don't think about how you will have to follow it for months. Just think about it day by day, meal by meal.

Sensory Material

Sensory material refers to things like music, traffic noise, and background chatter. This "clutter" can interfere with your ability to focus and get the job done. They provide distractions that can stress your brain.[29]

Try to keep things as quiet as possible while you work. Have a private area if you can and minimize noise with ear plugs, noise canceling headphones, or thick walls. Thick curtains can block out light and outside distractions.

Does music really pose a distraction? Study results are mixed. Many studies have found that music can actually enhance your concentration, because it actually reduces stress and negative emotions that can distract or overwhelm you.[32] It also encourages order and structure, two things you know your brain needs to be productive and self-disciplined.[32] Last but not least, it can ease burnout and make you enjoy your work or studying more.[32] There is a reason that music therapy works so well. Playing some music probably will not distract you to the point that you can't work efficiently anymore.

Why Do You Lack Motivation and Drive?

What do you do to motivate yourself? Motivation can be elusive, especially when you are doing something you hate. Your brain does not like doing things it hates because it wants instant gratification – in other words, it wants to be rewarded *immediately*.

There are a few ways to gain motivation that make your brain kick into high gear:

Do something meaningful. It is true that your brain seeks a deeper meaning or purpose in everything. This is indicated by patternicity, the strange way that your brain attempts to find patterns, such as making smiley faces out of dots on the ceiling.[33] Your brain likes to find connections, patterns, and meaningful depth in its surroundings. It wants to see your life's work connect to your goals and dreams. If you keep doing things that seem pointless, your brain quickly shuts down and gets burned out. Thus, you should focus on work and lifestyle changes that actually bring you joy and help you go where you want in life.

Do something fun. Making work more fun is a good way to skirt around the boredom issue that many people face.[23] Chat with your colleagues, make jokes to yourself, play basketball with the trash can. These little things can make a big difference in how motivated you feel and how much you want to go to work.[24] If you are trying to implement overall lifestyle changes, try to choose fun workouts that you actually enjoy and eat fun foods that follow the diet plan you choose. You may also gain more fun if you involve socializing in your routine.

Take lots of breaks. Breaks from work of any kind sort of jumpstart and refresh your brain. In fact, a movement break has been found to be the most beneficial.[34] Get up and stretch in the middle of working to reset your brain and improve your mental and physical health. A long walk to see new things is even better.

Snack breaks give you little rewards, though you should avoid eating too many calories to stave off weight gain.

Have small rewards for yourself. When you accomplish something, it's time for a victory dance. Reward yourself in some small way for a job well done. This satisfies your brain's intrinsic desire for a reward of some kind. A reward could be something simple like pizza, or something huge like a vacation to Tahiti. You need to make your hard work pay off in small ways if you are working toward a larger long-term goal, in order to prevent burnout and motivation loss.

Why Do You Cripple Yourself with Perfectionism?

Perfectionism can actually be a huge killer of self-discipline. This may seem counterintuitive, since self-disciplined people often appear perfect. But the reality is, perfectionism causes self-doubt. It also causes you to be rigid and to fixate on tiny details, thus devoting more time to the unimportant things versus the things that truly matter. For these reasons, being a perfectionist can actually kill your self-discipline and make you less efficient at your work.

Relaxing and being flexible are two key traits in successful people.[22] A big part of self-discipline involves relaxing enough to give your brain a break because anxiety doesn't do anyone any good. You must take some time to compose yourself. You must roll with the punches, as well, to avoid further stress.

When you try to be perfect or rigid, you really kill your motivation and drive by stressing your brain out far too much. Your brain cannot live up to your high standards and you spend too much time trying to correct tiny details. You set yourself up to fail.

Let's see how this would play out in real life. A good example is how a person who is on a diet may need to give himself a break now and then.[25] Another example would be Obama taking a break from official duties to play golf, which he credits for making him a better president.[22]

Chapter 4: How to Build and Increase Tolerance for Discomfort

A tolerance for discomfort may seem like an odd thing to talk about in a book about self-discipline. But the science behind human psychology proves that tolerating discomfort is a skill our brains naturally lack. This can make it hard to find the motivation to hold out for long-term rewards and to do things that are uncomfortable for some future good.

Let's face it: Work is uncomfortable. Whether you are working on your body with diet and exercise, or working on a degree, or working on some huge project at your job, you are in a state of discomfort as you work toward distant rewards without seeing them right now. As you learned above, willpower fails when you don't have anything motivating you. So get some motivation and learn to tolerate discomfort and you will be able to "trick" your brain into becoming self-disciplined.

Take a Cold Shower

A good trick to start building this tolerance for discomfort lies in taking a cold shower every morning. This is because cold showers are uncomfortable. The last thing you want to do after getting out of your cozy bed is step into a stream of icy water. However, making yourself do it is an act of self-discipline. You are forcing yourself to endure some discomfort for a greater long-term good. You are teaching yourself that doing things that you don't like will not kill you, which causes your brain to start to accept more uncomfortable things with less resistance.[8]

Change Your Thinking

You can effectively change your thinking, as decades of cognitive behavioral therapy has proved.[36] Changing your thinking drastically affects your mood and actions. By changing how you look at things, you can make situations less uncomfortable.

Of course, response rates to CBT vary based on a huge number of factors. For the most part, however, a study that analyzed over 269 metastudies pinpointed higher response rates to CBT than any other therapy.[36] The best part of this is that CBT is something you can practice yourself at home. Get high success without expensive therapy.

The core concept of CBT involves retraining your thinking to bring about different results in your attitude, behavior, and overall life. You are taught to identify problematic, or unhelpful, thinking in a journal. Then you are taught to replace these thoughts with more positive ones.

For instance, you might think, "I will fail." Jot this thought down in your CBT journal and then chase it with the thought, "I have succeeded before and I might succeed now if I try."

Through dedicated effort, you can change your thinking to stop focusing on the uncomfortable, the negative, and the hopeless. Thus, you will lift your mood and bring about more productive thinking and behavior. You will learn more about this in Chapter 9.

Look for Long-Term Rewards

As you embark on this new journey, a shift in thinking will make it easier to tolerate discomfort. From now on, you must look at situations from the outside and consider, "What is the cost versus benefit?" Consider any long-term rewards that will make the costs pay off.

Focusing on how you will benefit, or the reward, makes situations and work less uncomfortable. You will be able to tolerate unpleasant things, like getting up early, working late, missing game nights at your favorite bar, and sacrificing sleep, for something that you know will make it all worth it in the end.

Also, consider how working hard and succeeding proves to you your own worth and ability to get things done.[37] It isn't always about the money or the promotion. That is why people volunteer, to feel good about themselves instead of earning more money. Your own ego benefiting can be a huge reward to focus on.

The above information on CBT can help you start to retrain your brain to think this way.[36] Also consider this study that shows how you must focus on what you can bring to the table: Rosemary Batt, a doctoral candidate in labor relations and human-resource policy at MIT's Sloan School of Management, conducted research and discovered that employees who feel that their own skills are valued and being used tend to be happier and more productive.[37] This fascinating research shows that it isn't always money that you want – it's the reward of a job well done, by your own hands.

Avoid Considering Things from a Deprivation Standpoint

Since it is shown that human beings operate on a reward principle, it thus follows that people should not look at things from a deprivation standpoint. Deprivation is not something that the brain wants – or will tolerate. So when you look at things from the perspective that you are somehow losing something or missing out on something, you are setting yourself up for failure from the get-go.[23]

This principle is most commonly applied to dieting, but it can apply to any other goal or initiative. You focus on rewards and you get further. Don't think, "I can't eat this or that." Think, "I can eat this and that." When you consider how you win and what you can have, your brain sees this as a reward and accepts it. In other words – focus on the positive!

But there is another strange element at play here: The longer you wait to get a reward, the more deprived you tend to feel and the less sweet and satisfactory the reward is. This becomes uncomfortable. This is known as delay discounting.[38] All animals do it. But humans are willing to wait for months before discounting a reward, while other animals will discount it within seconds.[38]

Now that you know this, you can get a feel for why you lose steam when you have to wait too long or work too hard at something. You get discouraged, you lose interest, you lose patience. With this in mind, you can understand why working at a long-term goal is so difficult and often results in poor self-discipline.

This provides you with the perfect opportunity to remedy the problem. As you start to discount the delayed reward, find other rewards to focus on, to switch your brain from "deprived" to "satisfied." Celebrate small wins as well, so that you feel as if you are getting some part of the reward as you get closer to the end goal. Continue focusing on what you gain and not what you lose. Also be sure to take some time to enjoy yourself, so it's not all hard work and a sense of deprivation.[23]

There is nothing more counterproductive than looking back at the month behind you and thinking, "I just spent a hundred hours on this." That is discouraging and makes you feel deprived, as the reward still isn't here. Instead think, "I worked hard but I'm one hundred hours closer to the reward. It's still coming." Then treat yourself to drinks to celebrate your progress.

Stop Letting Moods Interfere

Stop believing everything you feel. Your moods are fleeting and fickle, making them unreliable figments of your imagination. Using them to make decisions is both irrational and dangerous. It will also kill your self-discipline, as you become a willing victim of your mood swings.

Humans have twenty-seven emotions.[39] Far more than the previously believed six. The study that found this out also labels emotions as "fuzzy," or not concrete.[39]

So with this evidence, do you really think listening to your bad mood or irritation is a good idea? Definitely not.

When it comes to your moods, understand that they will change in a few seconds. Stop banking your actions on how you feel in the moment. Also, stop basing your social interactions on your mood or how you feel about a person. To be self-disciplined, you must put your moods in the backseat and move on.

Not letting your moods run the show will increase your tolerance for discomfort exponentially. You won't focus on how uncomfortable you feel as much. You will be able to tolerate and ignore negative emotions in order to get things done.

The best way to do this is to tell yourself that your mood will change and then continue working. Another way is to try to change your mood with happy music or pictures that make you smile.

Avoid Temptation

Obviously, the brain is bad at resisting temptation. Talking yourself out of something tempting that appeals to you at a primal level is not very effective. So, to work around the problem of temptation, just avoid it altogether.[12]

Avoid the people who encourage you to procrastinate. Avoid watching your favorite program for hours and losing sleep. Avoid the desk with the candy bowl or donuts. Avoid the restaurant where you want to overeat.

It is easier said than done, of course. If your main temptation is smoking and your co-workers smoke, you are subjected to your temptation all of the time. Just the odor can trigger cravings. Or if someone brings donuts and leaves them in the common area, it is hard to walk by the box without sampling one. These are just examples, but you know firsthand how difficult resisting temptation can be.

Therefore, you should find workarounds, or replacement behaviors. These are behaviors you engage in when you run into one of your temptations. An example is chewing gum or eating sunflower seeds when you become tempted to smoke. Eating a special low-calorie dessert you brought from home when everyone else is eating donuts can help you avoid caving into the junk food.

The brain needs something to replace its temptations with so that it feels like it is receiving a reward of some kind. Otherwise, it feels deprived, which makes staying motivated to resist temptations even more difficult. With time, replacement behaviors can become habitual, lessening the severity of the cravings and temptation that you feel. Then it becomes less uncomfortable to resist cravings.

Chapter 5: The Impact of Environment and Relationships on Self-Discipline

Your surroundings greatly influence who you are and how you act. If you want to see change, you often have to be that change. In other words, you need to alter your environment and relationships to reflect the self-disciplined person you want to be. Holding into environments and relationships that do not nurture that sort of attitude will cause you to remain stuck in a vortex of struggle and failure.

There is concrete science behind this. Nim Tottenham, a professor of psychology at Columbia University, states implicitly that your amygdala is involved in emotional associations and maintaining vigilance on your surroundings.[35] It also works with the prefrontal cortex, regulating how aroused it becomes by situations.[35] Therefore, your brain is on the constant lookout for emotional events, which are heavily influenced by social relationships and your lifestyle. Its learning is thus altered based on your emotional experiences.

Albeit, the correlation between the two is stronger when you are an adolescent, Tottenham says. But there is still a tie between the prefrontal cortex and amygdala as you grow older. You may not have your feathers ruffled by things that happen around you as much, but you still do.

The verdict is that your emotional input can affect your brain. If you are trying to become more self-disciplined and you don't know what is stopping you, take a look at the emotional experiences you have and the models you use. The people you surround yourself with have tremendous influences on you and should be considered when you are evaluating your life.

Who Is There For You?

Before you delve into identifying and cutting off toxic people who drain your motivation, it is a good idea to look at the people who are there for you. You avoid a deprivation viewpoint when you focus on what you do have versus what you don't.

Identifying the people who are healthy for you to be around can be broken into a few key points:

They support you. A supportive friend both accepts and tries to help you on your journey. He or she offers words of encouragement and even advice. He or she does not actively try to sabotage your efforts and remains conscious of how he or she can help.

They accept you. A friend who is healthy for you accepts you as you are. He or she does not try to change or criticize you. If you take on a venture, he or she appreciates that.

They have good habits. We tend to build our behavior off of models. These models are the people we surround ourselves with. Healthy models are people who emulate the lifestyle and self-discipline you wish to achieve. Observing how they do it will encourage you to do it yourself. Your brain will want to copy their habits, thus building good habits of its own.

So who in your life is a healthy influence? Make a list to make it more solid and real. Writing things down tend to make them stick in your brain more.

Eliminating Toxins

In this context, toxins refer to the people and situations that prevent your personal growth. View each person or situation that poses a hurdle to your growth as a toxin that needs to be expelled from your life. Seeing them in this light helps you let go of the emotional attachment that causes you to cling to them.

Change is never comfortable for any human being. We have a natural, deep-seated fear of the unknown and a need for familiarity. As you have gotten used to your life, you have developed neural pathways that make you view each thing you are used to as a part of itself. For instance, your route home from work has become easy and you no longer get lost, because the roads have practically been paved into your mind.

When you make a change, you are upsetting these neural pathways, forcing them to rework themselves into new patterns. This makes your brain work, and you already know how your brain would really prefer not to work if it can.

Removing the emotion from things is a good way to make change easier. Emotions are wired to memories.[35] This is why you get attached to people and things and experience great pain when you have to let them go. But it is really the sole way to rewire your brain and bring about change. Essentially the saying "Be the change you want to see" is dead on.

To ease the pain, you should detach yourself mentally from your emotional attachments through visualization. Imagine these people or things as toxins that you must expel to be well. Imagine how life will be without them in it and imagine how you will be just fine with a life free of bad people.

Visualizations have stunning power in changing your mindset. A study has found that stroke patients who imagine themselves getting well tend to have faster recoveries than those who don't do this.[40] Your brain tends to think of these visualizations as reality at some level.[40] It is poorly understood why it works this way, but years of anecdotal evidence indicates that it does. This could be because visualizations pair well with both your emotional and memory centers as you imagine what you really want.

Use visualizations generously to heal your own life, just like stroke victims can. Imagine getting rid of toxic influences. Imagine being self-disciplined and leading your best life. Imagine working hard without griping or quitting.

Creating a Fostering Environment

The other key to bringing about change and encouraging new discipline is to change your environment. Common sense says that if you want a new life, you must create a positive environment that fosters the changes you want to bring about. Otherwise, obviously, you will keep doing the same things and being oppressed by negative influences.

A fostering environment will enable you to be self-disciplined. It would include people and situations who are permissive and supportive of you getting up early to exercise, working hard, and possibly coming home late. It would be an environment where you are not surrounded by bad food, bad habits, and toxic traits. You know what a fostering environment looks like, so consider how to change your lifestyle to reflect that vision you have.

Chapter 6: How to Reach the Point Where Discipline Is Automatic

Thus far, you have learned how to work on your self-discipline. But this work is hard and you don't want to have to do it for the rest of your life. Never fear, it is more than possible to turn self-discipline into an automatic process that you no longer have to think about or work hard to accomplish.

Self-Discipline Is Like a Muscle

Like any muscle, the more you work it, the stronger it becomes. Self-discipline soon takes on a sort of momentum that makes it automatic.

Momentum is the sole way to make things automatic where you don't have to think about them. Momentum is the process by which successes stack on top of each other, making your brain essentially "roll" onto the next success.

For example, you will pick up momentum at work the longer you do a job. You develop a system. You start to learn from your failures and gain more and more success. As people come to trust your insight, you get more responsibility and more privilege. Pretty soon, work is easy and you don't have to think about every little thing you do because you have it down pat and the work you've done before helps create the work you have in front of you. [41]

Businesspeople love to talk about momentum. The most common consensus in the scientific community is that momentum teaches you that you can do it – so you do it![41] Psychological momentum is heralded as the key to continued success after one triumph.[41] By proving your abilities to yourself, you enable yourself to become motivated. In other words, you are working that muscle, making it stronger, making it more automatic.

Psychological momentum triggers a sense of self-efficacy and a better vision of yourself as a performer.[41] As your self-esteem rockets, so does your willingness to tackle bigger and more advanced tasks. So as you build momentum, you also build the scale of things you attempt.

Better performers simply tend to perform better throughout the course of their work, according to one study.[41] One bout of success seems to drive people to go after more success. It also improves one's confidence and comfort at work, leading to greater mood.[41]

So to use this to your advantage, work hard at one goal until you achieve it. That success will provide you the basis to create your own psychological momentum, which is critical for your future goal pursuance and achievement.[41] Once you reach another goal, your brain is on a roll. Keep doing this, stacking achievements on top of one another, to reach a momentum that creates automatic success and the self-disciplined actions that bring about that success.[41]

Habits Stick

With time, the brain starts to restructure itself to make learned skills easier and more automatic, in order to lessen its workload.[6] In oversimplified terms, the brain will rewire itself and create new neural pathways that allow for this skill to be automatic.[6]

Thus, self-discipline is a habit that you can develop over time. Once you develop the habit, it is a part of you, literally. It has been wired into your brain and is no longer something you have to work hard on.

The key here is to keep practicing self-discipline and good habits that you learn along the way. The end result is a habit that sticks. It will become a part of your daily life and infuse your every action.

Start by forming a good routine that you can follow. Introduce bits and pieces of new behavior gradually. For instance, introduce morning exercise, or start waking up fifteen minutes earlier each morning. This routine helps you build the habits that allow you to follow the routine every day and stay disciplined in your efforts in all areas of life.

Chapter 7: The Function of Dopamine

Honestly, we are all slaves to dopamine; even the most disciplined people are slaves to its awesome power over human emotion and action. Dopamine is an incredibly powerful chemical that totally changes and elevates our moods. We do a lot of the things we do just to feel that dopamine rush. Dopamine is part of a complex chemical cocktail that drives how we feel, how we act, and basically who we are.

Dopamine is addictive for a reason. It gives you that euphoric rush to throw your fists in the air and shout, "yes!" Coupled with serotonin, which is that warm fuzzy feeling you get when you see your crush or a cute dog, it is can create a lot of pleasure. Meanwhile, norepinephrine makes you want to act *right now*. It can play a role in frenzies excitement, or in delirious panic.

Dopamine is ultimately just a chemical released by neurotransmitters within the brain that interacts with different receptors within synapses.[42] Dopamine hits many synapses and triggers many pathways in the brain, but the nigrostriatal and mesolimbic pathways within the brain are the ones that seem to primarily relate to rewards and motivation.[42] When you want to get disciplined and motivated, you need dopamine tickling these pathways. It gets a lot more complex, beyond the scope of this book, but understand that you can get dopamine flowing in regards to tasks to bring about motivation, inspiration, and self-discipline.

Dopamine is often what triggers the release of epinephrine, or adrenaline, which in turn triggers you to take action.[42] Your mesolimbic system will flood your synapses with dopamine *before* it gets a reward and floods you with epinephrine, meaning that dopamine's main function is to get you to act for a reward or to avoid something that could curtail your survival.[42] This is all part of the fight-or-flight reflex, but also part of the reward system hardwired into your brain. The short of all this is that dopamine is a reward-fueled neurochemical that drives you to act.[42]

Hence, it is a great idea to use dopamine to your advantage. You can manipulate it to give yourself the motivation necessary to do certain tasks that require self-discipline because they, well, don't naturally give a dopamine rush. Can you imagine getting a big dopamine rush before you do a heap of paperwork on Monday morning? It would be nice, wouldn't it? But it doesn't naturally happen because there is nothing intrinsically exciting or dramatic about paperwork. This is the essence of "tricking" your brain that this chapter is meant to teach you.

Where Dopamine is Problematic

Yes, there are some things that dopamine can make you do that is not very conducive to self-discipline. Understanding this first can help you learn how to use it to your advantage. It can also teach you to avoid the bad side effects of this natural drug produced within your own body.

The very first interesting discovery in testing rats is that dopamine is more sustained and thus more effective at changing behavior in rats that are conscious versus those that are anesthetized.[42] Why this happens remains a scientific head-scratcher, but what we can take away from this is that you must be awake and present to utilize dopamine. It takes effort and concentration to control it yourself. But as we already know, work is not necessarily motivating or enjoyable, so this very fact can make manipulating dopamine within your own brain tricky.

The other problem is that dopamine is hard to resist. You want to do things that release immediate rewards. So when you see that donut, your mesolimbic system floods your synapses with dopamine in preparation for the anticipated pleasure you will gain from eating it. You are already motivated to do something you probably shouldn't do – without even trying! It is an automatic process that you have trouble controlling.

The way around this is to learn how to make your dopamine start flowing as you work on long-term goals, doing unpleasant tasks that don't trigger dopamine waterfalls within your skull. That way, you aren't dreading work as badly, and you aren't as helpless to its pull when faced with some instantaneous but brief reward like chocolate.

Finally, dopamine rushes that can cause distractions. Many of our willpower failures (e.g., checking email excessively) are simply us pointlessly trying to get a reward because of a rush of dopamine. We get that rush when we hear a trigger like, "You've got mail!" We go after that trigger, even though it is something small. Learning to block out these triggers and wait for a more opportune time to, say, check email is all part of a habit that you develop with good time management, routine, and long-term reward concentration.

How to Use Dopamine to Your Advantage

When you are not self-disciplined, you don't have an automatic ability to drive yourself to act, even when the work isn't fun or pleasant. You have trouble delaying gratification because you are a slave to the dopamine that makes you want something *now*. You have the same amount of dopamine as the self-disciplined entrepreneur in your family that you envy – you just don't use it the right way.

To bring about a greater focus on long-term rewards and commitment to action even when it isn't instantly rewarding, you must learn to get your dopamine flowing about these things. There are a number of tricks to do this, which include being more social with your endeavors, celebrating small wins, and focusing on visualizations.

How to Grow Dopamine

Your body produces a finite amount of dopamine. It is what it does with this dopamine that is so critical. Keeping lots of dopamine in your synapses by limiting reuptake by your neurons is a good way to ensure that dopamine remains in your system, doing its work.

Here are some simple ways to trigger this abundance of dopamine:

- Use a to-do list. Each time you check something off, you can reward yourself with a pat on the back. These little accomplishments make you feel complete and accomplished. Cue dopamine release.
- Share results with others. Being social triggers dopamine and serotonin, two feel-good chemicals that give you the energy to reach a reward.[24] You can use this to your advantage by being more social about your goals and work. Talk about how well you've done and let others congratulate you.
- Take part in team efforts. Again, social pleasure is at play here.[24] You may enjoy sharing results with a team and getting things done with more than one pair of hands. The camaraderie, divided workload, and other benefits of

thinking with a team can all help, as well. On the other hand, if you are a loner and hate people, this tip may not work well for you and working alone will release the dopamine you need to crush your tasks.

- Use micro-deadlines for small tasks. As you reach smaller deadlines, you create that psychological momentum that is so wonderful. You prove to yourself that you can get things done and you feel more successful, which boosts your self-esteem.[41] You also break the task into smaller chunks that are easier to get done bit by bit, making the scope of the overall project smaller.

- Visualize the end result. How will you feel? How will you enjoy your life more? How will you or your loved ones benefit? These visualizations will seem real to your brain, encouraging you to feel as if you are already experiencing these rewards. That will trigger dopamine to be released as you bask in the pleasure of a job well done.

- Think back to why you started. Whatever your endeavor is, from losing weight to quitting smoking to starting a business, you started for a reason. Focusing on that reason and remembering your motivation can give you that little dopamine rush.

- Eat some probiotics. Probiotics tend to help your body produce more dopamine, such as yogurt, kefir, sauerkraut, kimchi, and pickled vegetables. This will also improve your digestion without messing up a diet. Probiotic pills can work too.

- Eat tyrosine. Chicken, fish, almonds, avocados, beans, bananas, and eggs are all sources of this stuff.

- Music can trigger dopamine. Listen to some as you work. This only works if you are listening to something you enjoy, though. A banjo track that grates on your nerves will likely have the opposite effect and kill your work ethic.

- A massage will release dopamine and serotonin. Even if you can't afford a daily massage, consider an ergonomic chair, or a massaging back mat on your chair. You can also stimulate sore, tired shoulders yourself to get a much-needed flood of dopamine in the middle of the workday.

- Take care of your body. Don't treat yourself like an afterthought. Self-disciplined people put their bodies first for good reason. When you get adequate sleep, water, nutrition, and exercise, your brain is able to function at optimal levels. That means more dopamine production for necessary tasks.

- Find small, fun things in your tasks. From trashcan basketball to finding the silver lining in things, you can seek out the joy in even the most trivial, boring tasks. Having fun with tasks will release feel-good neurotransmitters.

- Meditate. Give your mind a break when you start to feel bored, overwhelmed, or burned out. Take some time to meditate in solitude to renew your energy and focus. For some reason, meditation has been linked to dopamine release. You will feel better and have improved cognitive focus when you return to work.

Chapter 8: Habit and Routine Formation for Longer Lasting Behavior Modification

It is possible to rewire your brain to build good, lasting habits and routines that you follow by rote. As you observed in the chapter about successful self-disciplined people, people who are destined for greatness don't lead haphazard lives. They follow routines, which enable them to stick to their goals and achieve good results.

Routine is both comforting and authoritative to your brain. When you know what to do next, you don't have to waste time guessing or deciding what to do. You just do it. You have less trouble fitting things into your schedule and being flexible when you know the layout of your entire day. This is the exact reason that Mark Zuckerberg wears the same thing every day, to cut out the number of decisions he must spend time on.[13] Finally, you are less inclined to forget things because you already know what comes next.

Understanding Habits and Habit Loops

To create good habits and break bad ones, you first need to understand what happens inside your brain as habits form. Habits form when your brain creates a habit loop. The loop starts with a trigger that tells your brain to let the behavior happen. Next, your habit plays out in its routine way. Finally, the loop closes with the receipt of some reward. It's conditioning at its finest and it occurs all the time in your basal ganglia, a part of your brain that acts in memory making and pattern recognition.[48]

The main problem is that you make decisions in your prefrontal cortex.[48] This means that your decision making is not involved in your habits.[48] Once something gets committed to habit, it becomes automatic and the decision part is taken out. This is a good thing in that you can make behavior automatic, but it's bad in that it makes bad habits quite hard to break.

To become self-disciplined, you want to develop habits that let you accomplish great things. You want to create good habits for self-care, work, and family, as well as anything else you care about and want to succeed at. The best way to start this, however, is to start today by engaging in behaviors. Read on to learn how to condition your brain to create a habit loop.

Condition Your Own Brain

Let's talk about conditioning a bit. What good is all of this knowledge if you can't make it stick for the long-term? To truly become self-disciplined, you must take these new habits and make them long-lasting. That means uprooting old thinking patterns and habits to bring about newer, better ones. One way to do this is through these two types of conditioning.

I still feel guilty when I eat two cookies after supper, even as an adult, because as a child I was never allowed to have more than one after dinner. If I ate more than one, I'd get punished. This proves how long-lasting operant conditioning you receive in childhood can be and the deep impression it makes upon your mind. You don't just need to get this conditioning in childhood, however. You can start at any time in life and have lasting results.

There are two types of conditioning: operant and classical. Operant conditioning is defined as associating an action with a consequence.[47] The consequence could be negative, such as a punishment, or it could be positive, such as a reward. Most learning we do in life comes from operant conditioning. A child learns not to take a second cookie after dinner for fear of getting grounded, for instance.

Meanwhile, classical conditioning uses two stimuli.[47] One might be a bell ring, for instance, which triggers a behavior. Then the other is a stimulus that presents when a reward is presented. The result is a cemented idea of what to do when you hear a stimulus. Pavlov first used this form of conditioning on dogs.

To really form a habit, you must teach your brain what the habit is. Then you can teach your brain a stimulus, or trigger, that makes your brain do the action in question automatically once you hear that stimulus. In Pavlov's case, bells were used. You don't have to use that, however. You can use something such as your morning alarm to trigger the acting out of a routine that you have carefully rehearsed and taught yourself. You could use meditation bells, which are designed to "transition" the brain into a meditative state but can be used to trigger any behavior you desire.

As you practice your new routine, you should also use operant conditioning, where you give yourself a reward for good behavior or a punishment for bad behavior. Every time you tick a task off of your to-do list or follow your routine to a T, reward yourself. Just the act of doing what you are supposed to do can create the dopamine rush you need for a feel-good reward.

Conditioning only works if it is used over a period of time. It also works when coupled with a reward for the desired behavior. To condition yourself, you must repeat the exercises several times and you must reward yourself somehow to make it worthwhile to your own brain. You are training yourself, just like a dog. It can be a surreal experience that is certainly worthwhile when you cement healthy, self-controlling habits.

Another consideration to bear in mind is that punishment doesn't work as well as rewards. Positive reinforcement will lead to greater results in operant conditioning.[47] Skinner found this out with rats, who were much more responsive to rewards for pressing on a lever than punishments.[47] If you want to truly modify your behavior, start to reward yourself for taking self-disciplined actions that you are proud of. Don't punish yourself for failing or you will actually backtrack in success, according to a lot of behavior research.

Rewards can be anything that gives you a little dopamine rush. A cheat meal when you have successfully followed a diet all week, a pizza party for your team when you hit a sales goal, a spa trip or vacation after a year of hard work, or just self-praise and self-love is sufficient to teach yourself that hard work and self-discipline will result in good things. Don't just hold out for the long-term rewards to avoid delay discounting.[38] But be sure to bask in them when they happen.

Form a Routine

A routine is best formed the night before. Write it down, to make it more physical and therefore real to your brain. Plan the whole day and how it will play out. Be sure to incorporate everything you need to do. A planner is especially helpful for this.

Next, act the routine out. Then plan again at night and repeat. This starts to make the routine habit. It also gives you positive reinforcement, as you notice how the routine helps you get more done and have better time management with less stress. As you begin to enjoy the routine, it starts to become habitual.

Another good idea is to start implementing one new habit into your routine every so many days. This makes the change light and easy to stick with. This is especially useful in lifestyle change, when people are stuck in unhealthy ways. So for one day, introduce an early morning yoga routine. Later one introduce twenty minutes of meditation before work. So on and so forth.

Using a friend can hold you accountable. Ask a friend to work out with you or ask your spouse to remind you of your routine. Having some social support can help you stick to the new routine and habits.

Create a System

Systems tie in with routines, though they are not the same. A system is an organized way of doing tasks that makes the work more streamlined. Successful people use systems to eliminate the amount of effort they must put in, allowing themselves to accomplish more and generate higher quality work.

Take your usual workday. A good system would involve a way to organize your office so that everything is within easy reach. Then you can create a system for your planner, so that you can organize your time throughout the day. Another system would involve how you take notes on your computer, utilizing different software programs to get your desired results. You will also create a communication system, where you know to email your boss the completed project the minute it is finished and double check to ensure the email went through.

Systems are much like the to-do lists and bite-sized chunks of goals that we have already discussed, but they take these things a step further. You get things done in an ordered and simple way that never varies. Systems are totally customizable based on your work ethic, skills, and available resources. Look at what you must accomplish and what you have at hand and work out your own systems. When you find a system that works, make it routine by using it every time you work on a particular task.

A good system will be totally easy. You don't have to think – it's all automatic. Find an ordered process that works by letting you transition from one part of the task to another. For instance, you might be working within a Microsoft Xcel document to create a new budget plan and you must use another window to gather information from the web. Then you must switch to your email to send the budget plan to your boss. Have all of these windows open and waiting behind each other so that you can switch between them smoothly and not have to think hard about what to do next. This system allows you to get work done faster, but also ensures that you don't forget any steps because it's all right there, serving as an automatic reminder.

Having a series of systems throughout the day lets you accomplish that routine that is so essential to being disciplined. When you have easy ways to get everything done, you cut down on your brain's workload. Your brain switches between the tasks at hand more smoothly, allowing you to get a lot done. This is the secret of those enviable people who appear to have more hours in the day than the rest of humanity. They don't have more hours, they just have an efficient routine of comprised of efficient systems.

Chapter 9: Top Scientific Ways to Build Self-Discipline

Up to this point, you have read how to improve your motivation, increase tolerance for discomfort, build psychological momentum, get dopamine flowing, build routines, and other mental tools to improve self-discipline. Now you will get into the meat of the book – the actual scientific ways that you can retrain your brain and change your behavior using these aforementioned tools. Various studies and psychology observations have provided the foundation for these foolproof techniques. Using the skills you have already built in previous chapters, you will be able to achieve great success with these methods.

Before you even begin learning about this stuff, however, you need to make up your mind what you really want to accomplish. What do you need self-discipline for? Keep these goals sharp in your mind as you tackle self-improvement using science-backed methods. Your goals will provide you with motivation to drive you through the tough parts when you want to give up. They will also give you resolve, something that the brain needs to stick to something, much like a hiker who conquers Mount Everest against unspeakable odds.

Write these goals down and refer back to them as you read this chapter. Start to formulate an action plan based on what you read here and what your goals are. For instance, if your goal is to open your own restaurant in the next five years, consider the steps you need to take to do that. Then consider what makes you lose self-discipline and how you can use things like habit formation, dopamine manipulation, and the like to achieve your desired result. Implement these tips at every step to create something you can actually do. Otherwise, there is no use reading books about self-discipline if you don't put the information into action. You will simply forget most of what you read and gain no benefit from it.

Use Cognitive Behavioral Therapy on Yourself

CBT is a therapeutic technique that changes your thinking, feelings, and actions all in one. Originally meant to treat depression and addiction, it can be used to teach self-discipline.[36] As the most successful type of therapy out there, you can rest assured it really will work on changing your mind. The best part is that you don't need to enroll in therapy. You can do CBT on yourself with splendid results.

CBT works when you use it on yourself simply because it utilizes mindfulness of your own thoughts coupled with thought redirection to bring about better, healthier mental strategies. You can accomplish it simply with a few mental tools and a journal.

To begin CBT, you first must analyze your thinking and your self-belief system. This is clear enough. A journal can help you; jot down your thoughts about a project or endeavor that requires self-discipline. You can pick out the different "cognitive distortions," or poor thinking, that you engage in that limits your self-discipline and self-efficacy.

Cognitive distortions are simply poor paths that your thoughts take, which cause negative results in your life. Aaron Beck first identified them in 1976 and David Burns popularized and solidified the concept in the 1980s.[43] Numerous cognitive distortions could lie at the heart of your lack of self-discipline[43]:

Filtering

You see and accept only the negative out of each situation. You filter out the positive. This makes your reality seem particularly dim. If you are filtering, you might focus on how everyone seems to hate you for being fat and never notice when people like you or are kind to you.

Polarized Thinking (or "Black and White" Thinking)

Things are black and white, all or nothing. You can't accept that there is a likely gray air in all things. You must have things one way or the other and freak out when you don't. This kind of thinking can make progress on any work hard because you expect one single result. Life doesn't work that way, though.

Overgeneralization

Many people are guilty of this one. This is where you draw a conclusion off of one tiny piece of evidence or one tiny isolated incident. You may assume that someone is a bad person because of one encounter, or you may think you are a failure because you failed once. This kind of thinking prevents you from seeing the bigger picture and moving on with life. It also drives you to snap judgments that may be wrong.

Jumping to Conclusions

This is a lot like mind reading – you assume what someone else is saying, thinking, or feeling without asking. You have a 50/50 shot at being right – and you may be wrong. When you jump to conclusions, you assume the worst and operate on those assumptions as if you are sure they are true. This can lead to you making mistakes. It can also alienate people who care about you or who could help you on your path to success.

Catastrophizing

You expect the worst outcome possible. You make small things much bigger than they are. This fear of catastrophe and overdramatizing makes life unpleasant for you, resulting in you being afraid. For instance, if you are so afraid that your business will fail, then you will never even attempt to open it.

Another problem with catastrophizing is that you assign inappropriate proportions of blame. You may beat yourself up over something tiny, while dismissing a serious insult from someone else. This cripples your ability to gain respect in your social spheres and hurts your self-esteem.

Personalization

Personalization is when you assign far too much personal significance. You think everything everyone does is about you. This can make you very paranoid and easily enraged. Learning that the world isn't all about you and people have separate motives is essential.

Control Fallacies

In either fallacy, you feel controlled externally and helpless, or you feel that you have internal control over the entire world. Neither fallacy is true. You don't have complete control and should learn to be flexible so that you can work with problems when they arise. But you must also realize that you can direct your fate and change your life as you see fit. You aren't some puppet played by fate.

Fallacy of Fairness

This fallacy is where you think of how things should be fair and you are angry when they aren't. Teenagers are especially bad about this but adults can be too. You must start to realize that life isn't always fair, but you have the power to do something about that. Let your self-discipline help you make a difference in the world with your accomplishments. Control your emotions and work toward fairness.

Blaming

You blame another person for how you feel. You will tell someone, "You make me feel bad." Well, no one can make you do or feel anything, you do it to yourself. Learn to take accountability and control of your own feelings and impulses instead of putting them on another.

Should Thinking

Should thinking is always problematic because it lets you entertain a world that does not exist, thus making you feel horrible when you must face the real world. You always say "should" instead of seeing how things are. To be self-disciplined, you should acknowledge how things really are in order to work with them and use them as leverage to your own success.

Emotional Reasoning

This is the super common habit that people have of assuming their feelings must be true. For instance, if you feel left out or ugly, you assume you must be left out or ugly. You won't acknowledge evidence to the contrary. This cognitive dissonance causes you to act on fleeting emotions, something we have already talked about as a no-no in self-discipline.

Fallacy of Change

In this case, you assume someone will change to suit your needs if you just try hard enough. But people don't change. You end up stuck in toxic relationships, waiting for the other person to change out of love for you. You alienate people by pressuring them to be different than they are. To be self-disciplined, you must accept that other people are different and will not change for you. You must learn to give up useless pursuits and go after things that are more fruitful, or find clever workarounds to get your way.

Global Labeling

Global labeling is an extreme exaggeration of the qualities of yourself or another person. You use one tiny incident or trait and blow it out of proportion to make things sound worse than they are. For instance, if your business loses some money, you start to say, "I am going bankrupt!" You may also hate a whole race of people or homosexuals and call them foul names because something bad happened to you once a long time ago involving one such person.

Always Being Right

You have to be right, no matter what. You will argue and lose friends just assert your correctness. This is no way to be – especially as a self-disciplined person. Being right and not learning from your mistakes can eat away at your success as a self-disciplined person.

Heaven's Reward Fallacy

This one is a doozy. You think that the world owes you something. When you put work in or do the right thing, you expect a reward. But life doesn't always reward everything, or rewards may be far off in the distance, as you have already learned. Focusing on long-term rewards and not feeling entitled are keys to dropping the disappointment and disillusionment that arises with this fallacy of thinking.

How to Change Cognitive Distortions

You have learned about fifteen major cognitive distortions and how they can interfere with your success as a self-disciplined person. Now watch your thinking and see if you buy into any of these.

A good, simple exercise is to write in your CBT journal when you are upset. Write about the upsetting event, what you think about it, and if any of your thoughts are possibly fallacious. Look to see if your thoughts stand up to reason and logic, or don't hold water with hard evidence and sound reasoning. Then consider how you can think about the event differently without the different cognitive distortions. Record how your feelings change as you change your thinking.

For each cognitive distortion, there is a different way to look at the world. You can figure it out using common sense. For instance, if you are using emotional reasoning, you can say, "Are my feelings valid? Should I step back and look at this from a logical standpoint and push my emotions aside for now?" Or if you are using the term "should," stop that and rephrase your sentences to say something like, "This is how it is, but this is how I want it to be. I will work hard to change things."

Regulate Self-Talk

Self-talk is another huge part of CBT. It details how you need to talk to yourself in a manner that furthers your desired goals and makes you feel better. How you talk to yourself has been shown to change your mood, according to research.[44] It can regulate and influence your mood significantly. Your dialogue with yourself seems to have as much weight as a chat with someone else, and thus changes how your brain views itself. In fact, third-person self-talk appears to have even more of a profound effect on your brain.[44]

To gain more self-discipline, talk to yourself in a way that encourages that, and teach your brain to embrace self-discipline. Tell yourself things like, "I can do that," or "How can I do that?" instead of "I can't do that" or "I don't know how to do that." Just these little changes will adjust how your brain perceives tasks and can even give you that much-needed jolt of dopamine for performance.

Another helpful trick involving self-talk is to praise yourself to give yourself some dopamine and serotonin. Praise yourself for working hard. Take responsibility for your actions by saying, "I did all this!" The swell of pride you feel is an incredibly strong motivator.

Alter Your Schemas

Schemas are another part of cognitive behavioral therapy. Like cognitive distortions, schemas refer to long-held patterns that you believe about yourself and the world around you.[49] But unlike cognitive distortions, schemas are often hidden in your subconscious mind, influencing your thoughts without any clear correlation.[49] They are often the root of why you adopt certain cognitive distortions and why you act the way you do. As you take in information from the world, you distort it according to your personal schema and then decide how to act based on that.[49]

Schemas can be different for everyone. But they usually form in early childhood and follow you through adulthood. They give your brain a framework by which it can understand itself.[49] That's all well and good, until you consider that you might be operating based on a negative schema your entire life. That schema could be the core reason you lack motivation, drive, and follow-through. Changing it could enable you to become the self-disciplined individual you yearn to be.

You can identify your schemas based on how you feel about the world and what your automatic thoughts are. For instance, if your boss calls you into his office, what's your first thought? Is it "I'm about to be fired" or "I think I might be getting a raise!"? Your first thought can reveal a lot about your general worldview. This worldview is what ideas like optimism, pessimism, and realism are referring to.

A common schema that undermines self-discipline is the belief that you have no control and Fate is battering you around. You naturally won't take control or action if you feel that everything is out of your hands. Another schema is the belief that the world is a cruel place and it's out to get you. You probably won't try to succeed and be disciplined if you feel that someone or something is going to rip it all away from you one day. Maybe your schema is that you always fail and can't do anything right and the world doesn't help matters, or you believe you are not worthy of anything great because you did something bad or were told you were a bad person early in childhood. All of these schemas have detrimental effects on your ability to develop self-discipline.

Figure out what your schema is by analyzing your thoughts and common cognitive distortions for a while in your CBT journal. Pay special attention to the automatic thoughts that pop into your head without any effort on your part. Then start to change these schemas by forcing yourself to think along more positive lines. Chase the automatic thoughts with more positive ones and this will slowly but surely rewire your brain to adopt a different worldview. This can help you strengthen your resolve to build great self-discipline and thrive at anything you endeavor to do.

Building Psychological Momentum

In an earlier chapter, you learned how beneficial and helpful psychological momentum is. But you only got an overview of what it is and how it works. Now you will learn how to build this momentum and use it to become a self-disciplined god.

Psychological momentum is built primarily upon the back of one success. You just need that one win to get you going on a roll of achieving more wins. But how do you reach that one stage of success? And what about the sophomore slump or the "yips," when you are highly successful for a streak but suddenly run out of steam and start messing up? How do you keep momentum going in that case?

The first step is to take control of certain areas of your life. Having some control can give you the sense of confidence that lets you build on top of your accomplishments, even if you haven't hit a big win yet. Take control of your finances and start to increase your credit, or get a gym membership, or start eating just one clean meal a day. Even just taking care of one task on your to-do list, such as a home improvement project, can make you feel good. These are little ways to get control back.

What is really interesting is that your brain perceives control over your life in an odd way. Your brain wants control over its environment – very, very badly.[45] But when it lacks this control, it will suffer. A study suggests that control and desired outcomes are not just a desire, but a "biological necessity."[45] No wonder you feel so depressed when things don't go your way. Taking control in very small ways still gives your brain that feeling it utterly craves.

Next, figure out what is draining your energy. We talked about this in Chapters 3 and 6. Only when you eliminate sources of lethargy, toxins, and bad habits do you make the room for greater ones. You must clean out your life in order to build momentum. Doing this also gives you some control, as well. That is a second win to build that momentum on top of.

Consider how much energy and time you devote to things that don't serve you. Maybe you spend time with people who bring you down, or you take part in workplace activities and party planning that robs you of valuable you time. These things are taking up space in your life and cluttering your brain with thoughts and information, without serving any purpose or fetching any reward. Time to let them go.

The final step is to get organized and create a system at work. Consider the CEO who color codes his schedule. It may seem rather Type A, but it works. Get organized, to appeal to your brain, and see how life gets smoother. Since your brain loves being organized, this step works. It provides the logical order within chaos that you need to feel in control.[45] The end result is that you had a smooth playing field to start working and gaining momentum without clutter getting in the way.[25]

Now what about the slump you may experience? People may build momentum and then somehow falter and lose their footing. It happens more frequently than you realize. Consider Momofuku Ando, a Japanese businessman who is famous for the invention of instant ramen. Before he become rich and famous, he operated a merchandising firm and was highly successful. Then he was convicted of tax evasion and spent two years in prison. Meanwhile, his business went bankrupt. That's a pretty bad fall from success and a total stall of momentum. But he still got back on his feet. Humans are nothing if not resilient.

When you find momentum lapses in your life, all you can do is pick up the pieces and start over. Start small, with the organization and cutting out bad people and creating systems that work in your life. Clear the way for big success. Use this as a chance to recharge your brain with dopamine and adrenalin, in preparation for big change.

For some reason, the brain gets a surge of energy and renewed vigor when faced with failure or disaster and the chance to start anew. It is sort of the same reason that starting a diet or exercise program on a Monday, the beginning of a new week, is usually more successful than starting on any other day.[10] The reason for this is that your brain sees this as a clean slate and a new opportunity, which can be refreshing. When you get stuck, sometimes a fresh beginning is all you need to get your brain kicked into high gear again.[10]

Using Social Leverage

To become self-disciplined, it can pay off handsomely to use other people to get to where you want to be. A good technique in building self-discipline is using others for motivation and dopamine/serotonin release. You can also use networking as a means to further yourself and broaden your horizons, which certainly helps in your efforts to become self-disciplined. Having a happy social life is essential for your creativity and work ethic, as well.

Socialization as Self-Discipline

Socializing in and of itself is an act of self-control.[46] Think about it. You have to smile and be polite when a person is boring you. You have to think of relevant topics, even if they don't interest you, just to keep the conversation going. You must always think before you speak and restrain yourself from utter rudeness. All of these things require self-discipline and concentration, as you ignore your animal urges to behave "appropriately."

Erving Goffman actually uses theatrical drama to illustrate the point that socialization is playing a part in a complex play involving many characters.[46] Each person must know a role and play a part.

Therefore, engaging in social interaction is a good way to train yourself and gain practice as a self-disciplined person. Learning to engage with others in a polite way is also an incredibly useful and powerful skill to possess as life goes on. You will find it comes in handy when you need connections to get ahead, to provide references, or to network you into new opportunities.

Learn some etiquette, or in other words, learn how to play your unique part in the play of socializing. It is the very essence of self-control. Then use it in social settings as you attend networking events and take part in sites like LinkedIn, or other themed sites for professionals in your field. These things will help get you out there and help you forge meaningful connections that are far more conducive to your success than the toxic friendships you have learned to let go of.

Learn from Your Part

How you present yourself to the outside world has a very real effect on how you see yourself internally. This is related to the fact that your brain sees yourself reflected in others.[46] The result is that it learns to see and mimic the behavior that it notices in this reflection.

This plays in with the adage "Fake it till you make it." NLP, or neurolinguistics programming, is a controversial pseudoscience that aims to change your mindset through your actions. It firmly believes that you can change yourself simply by changing your speech, body language, and social interaction. It advocates faking it till you make to teach yourself confidence, openness, seductiveness, and charisma. Whether this is true or not, there is little doubt that how you present yourself to the world has a big influence on who you become and how you feel about yourself. It makes others treat you differently, affecting how you treat yourself.

Thus, being grandiose and self-disciplined in your impression is a good way to become that way in real life.[46] You see yourself act this way and want to maintain the façade in real life, until it isn't a façade anymore. You also feel pressure to keep up your impression to avoid letting people you meet down. If you present yourself as a self-disciplined person at the first meeting, the last thing you want to do is reveal yourself to be the opposite later on. That's a good way to ruin friendships and lose jobs.

Use Fear of Disappointing Others

People are very afraid of disappointing others. This can be a social leverage point that you can use to convince yourself to use your very best behavior and operate at your peak performance in order to please. The end result will be that you act in self-disciplined ways and meet goals to avoid unpleasant social repercussions, such as embarrassment.[10]

Use this to your advantage. Make a big promise to your boss or client, and then meet it. This can create the win you need to grow your confidence, create momentum, and start self-discipline habits that carry through to other projects. You will follow through because you don't want to actually let anyone down or lose your job.

Family and friends can be a huge factor in this, as well. You don't want to let them down at all. They can hold you accountable and make you feel guilty when you don't do what you were supposed to. This is the idea behind workout buddies or diet buddies.

Use Others for Personality Change

If you are not self-disciplined, then that is a change you want to make in your personality. You probably don't want to become a perfect Type A and give yourself a heart attack.[1] Nevertheless, you can and should start to develop more self-discipline. But did you know that being around other people can help you bring about personality change?

Research shows that your social investment can actually adjust your personality traits.[4] If you want to change badly enough, you will. You can grow your extraversion and other Big Five personality traits the more you are socially invested in work and interact with co-workers. Thus, being around people who make you more self-disciplined is good for your overall self-discipline in time.

Use Comparisons and Competition

A lot of motivational self-help books will drill this idea into your head: Don't compare yourself to others. This may be sound advice in many ways, but actually comparing yourself to others may just influence you to adopt the traits you envy in them. Just as tax letters comparing tax evaders to others who do pay their taxes were effective, any kind of social comparison can successfully drive you to be your best.[10] You want to measure up or even beat other people. You will derive a *huge* dopamine rush from that success.

Comparison is the basis for competition. You want what someone else wants. You must compare yourself to him or her to measure weaknesses and assess what your chances are. Competition drives you to perform at your best so that you can win, hands down.

Compare yourself to other colleagues who may be getting promotions or pay increases while you don't. See how they work and what they do that you don't. Then mold your work habits after theirs to see if you can achieve the success they do. Chances are, these people are self-disciplined, motivated, and able to churn out really high quality work. You can learn to act that way by trying to match or even beat them, so that you can become better and get the next raise or promotion for yourself.

Make Your To-Do List Better

If a standard to-do list doesn't inspire you, then a revamped one can. As you already know, checking off items on a to-do list gives you a little dopamine rush as you sense accomplishment. However, if a to-do list simply bores you, or you create one and then don't refer back to it and therefore don't accomplish anything on it, what is the use? It is possible to get more out of your to-do lists by tricking your brain into taking it more seriously.

The brain remembers images better than ordinary writing.[50] A vividly visual to-do list can trick your brain into remembering the contents better. You might use pictures or color coding to make it more visually appealing. Also, your brain much prefers little designs, such as fleur-de-lis, instead of bullet points for this same reason.[50] Avoid large chunks of text, as your brain doesn't bother remembering that at all.[50]

The more specifically you word things, the better. "Meeting" is pretty vague. But "Meeting with John about the merger" is a bit more on point and stands out more. Your brain will remember things with more details.

But there's a caveat: Too many written details and your brain will go the opposite way and forget.[50] This is because your brain does not have the desire to store a ton of information that it doesn't view as useful and it loses interest when staring a big block of boring text. This categorizing information process goes on automatically and it beyond your control, which is why you need to understand your own brain and trick it to remember the things you want. So keep your to-do list tasks short and sweet, with enough details to help you remember.

Structure your to-do list chronologically so that you give yourself a clear order of events throughout the day. This is the order your brain craves. Start with your first morning task and move on to your last. It is helpful to plan your day the night before, when you know what you need to get done. Throughout the day, check it and mark off completed tasks.

In some cases, chronological order does not necessarily work because you have many tasks to do and no real timely order in which you must do them. In this case, assigning priority is helpful. Use a highlight color or some sort of symbol to mark high, medium, and low priority. Start on high priority first and then work your way down. Low priority can wait. Update the priority every night. For instance, maybe returning that email isn't top priority today, but you can't ignore it forever, so tomorrow it might turn into high priority because you have to reply to it within a reasonable time frame.

There is always that one unpleasant task on your to-do list, the one that takes the most self-control. It could be working out, or making a phone call to a rude person, or giving someone bad news. Highlight or mark this worst task and get it done before your lunch break. That gives you both a deadline and a clear ability to get it done. Unpleasant tasks are high priority simply because you dread them and put them off. Getting them over, like ripping off a Band-Aid, is a huge act of self-discipline and a true accomplishment. The relief you feel when you get it done should be the reward you need to stay motivated.

A reflection at the end of the day gives you a true sense of accomplishment. When you have check things off of the to-do list, look over it and praise yourself for a job well done. Write down three big highlights that you accomplished within the last 24 hours. Also reflect on how these tie into bigger goals and how much closer you are to your end goal.

Meditate on Being Disciplined

Meditation has been shown to positively enhance the self-control and mental strength of stroke victims.[16] And the fact many CEOs swear by it is encouraging, since CEOs are some of the most disciplined people you will ever meet. Therefore, you should try using meditation to enhance your mental strength and self-discipline from within.

Transcendental and mindfulness meditations appear to be the two must effective forms.[16] You can attend a class or download an app with a variety of meditations in order to learn how. Meditating allows you to escape the real world to travel deep within your mind, while relaxing your body completely and taming unwanted, intrusive thoughts. As you spend time in this state, you start to gain more control over your mind and you can learn to control thoughts as they enter your mind. This can help you in the real world, when you start to think something that will derail your self-discipline. Just tell the thought to go away.

You can also engage in self-hypnosis while meditating. When you are meditating, your brain is very much in tune with itself. You can repeat to yourself, "I will get this done" and let it sink into your mind's subliminal depths. When you wake back up, the idea that you will get something done has been planted into your brain. This practice is of some controversy in the science world, but many people claim it works for them.

Adopt a New Mindset

This section ties in with the CBT section on changing your thinking. But here you will learn some more specific information about *how* to change your mindset. You will find these mindsets much more helpful in regulating self-control and building self-discipline because they present your brain with the option that something is possible.

You defeat yourself when you have a negative attitude. As you think something won't work, your brain hears that message and doesn't even bother trying as a result. But reverse that and consider how a "can-do" approach in your thinking can encourage you to actually make an effort.

It all goes back to that self-talk. When you are presented with a problem, ask, "How can I fix this?" as opposed to bemoaning your bad luck or assuming it's time to quit. When you feel hurt, ask "Why do I feel this and what can I do about it?" instead of giving into your feelings and letting them dictate your actions. And finally, when you come up with an idea, ask, "How can I implement this and make it reality?"

These simple self-questions change your whole mental approach. You start to open up your creativity, thinking of solutions and steps, instead of automatically giving up and shutting down. Plus, you create a little dopamine zap when your brain senses that action is about to be necessary. That feels good and drives you to activity.

Practice Self-Monitoring

You are the only person who can keep yourself in check. Your boss can try, but he's not with you 24/7. It's the same with your parents, your spouse, and anyone else who assumes control over you. Ultimately, at the end of the day, it's you who is in charge of your choices, your actions, and even your feelings.

Therefore, self-monitoring can be quite instrumental in developing self-discipline. It is useful to monitor your accomplishments and progress toward each goal. Using milestones or graphs can appeal to your brain in a more visual fashion than simply writing down, "I'm this much closer to my goal."[50]

When making decisions, pause and think how it affects your progress. Self-monitor what you give your time to. Things that are not important are simply distractions.

Build Motivation

Here's a formula for those of you who prefer math over words: Value * Likelihood.[51] In other words, if something matters to you, you are more likely to do it. Your brain is like the proverbial donkey: it must see a carrot at the end of the stick in order to want to plod forward.

To get motivated to do things, even things that are unpleasant, you must care about the end result. That is why you should set up huge end goals that actually matter to you on a deeply personal level.[51] Otherwise, you won't see the logic in putting a huge effort into something that means very little to you.

Rewards can be as simple as cake. The little dopamine rush of pleasure that comes from binging on a delicious food item is still a little dopamine rush of pleasure to your brain. It counts for something. However, rewards don't always have to be that small. Especially when working hard toward a long-term goal that is not paying out in the short term, motivation can run dry. Having a deeply personal, emotional reason behind your desired goal is a good way to keep yourself running toward the end without delay discounting.[51]

Some of the best motives are social. You might want to please your family, provide better for your kids, or impress your parents. You might also want to prove wrong the people who doubted your ability to succeed. All of these are good motives that provide delicious satisfaction and tons of dopamine when you complete your goals.

Other good motives include increasing your satisfaction with yourself. In fact, that's a huge motivator for most people. Losing weight, getting healthier, finishing college, getting a dream job, opening your dream restaurant – these are all goals that involve pleasing yourself.

Yet another good motive is making amends. You might have defaulted on a loan, had a falling out with a family member, or done something else you feel guilty about. Your subsequent actions are an attempt to make up for and atone for your mistake. This is why a lot of addicts and alcoholics get sober eventually and go through the twelve steps, which includes apologizing to hurt family and friends.

Find your deeply personal motive. Then figure out where to go from there. You will do it if you care about it enough.[51]

Conclusion

In just seven chapters, you have found the secrets to revolutionizing who you are. As you can see, self-discipline is essential to becoming the type of person who gets things done. Self-discipline will allow you to drive yourself to complete a challenge, lose weight, become healthier, end bad habits, and basically turn your life around.

For years, you may have felt that self-discipline was a special thing possessed by a shiny select few that eluded you. However, now you know that you can become self-disciplined yourself. It is just a skill that you must learn and turn into habit.

You can't use your personality type or genetics or chronic illness as an excuse to put off becoming self-disciplined. The truth is that you can change yourself with dedicated work. Your DNA and neural pathways will literally change as you work on new habits and routines.

You also can't use discomfort as an excuse anymore. Life is not always comfortable. You have learned how to endure the hardships and discomfort that can come with the hard work required for success. Using a long-term reward mindset, you will see the sacrifices as very necessary for the end results.

Using self-disciplined people as role models, you can actually teach yourself the secrets to self-discipline. Our brains tend to use models to create reality and behavior. Selecting the right models will change you for the better.

You can also use classical and operant conditioning to create lasting behavioral changes. You have learned how to do this and how to create healthy, helpful routines and habits that will guarantee you more success in life. Put these tips to work today and notice how your behavior improves.

CBT proves that there is a close link between your thinking, your emotions, and your behavior. By changing any one of these things, you change the other two. You will notice that as you modify your behavior, you will start to feel better and think along more productive lines. Then your improved and disciplined behavior will become easier and more automatic.

You will also find that practicing habits creates neural pathways in your brain that allow for more effortless self-discipline. It essentially will become a part of you the more you practice it. The saying "practice makes perfect" is fitting here.

Finally, you must change your life a bit to allow for more self-discipline. Certain people and environments are not conducive to success. Anything or anyone who holds you back should not remain in your life if you truly want to be self-disciplined. Making change is hard for any human, but focusing on rewards can help you get the dopamine rush you require to look forward to results.

With all of these tools, you are set for an amazing life. You will thoroughly enjoy the results that come from being a self-disciplined person. Your true potential can now be unlocked as you tackle larger and larger projects and prove more and more ability to yourself. So don't wait any longer. Start implementing these scientific-based tools today.

Thank you for reading!

References

1. Friedmann, Meyer & Rosenmann, Ray. (1974). *Type A Behavior and Your Heart.* Alfred A Knopf. ISBN-13: 978-0394480114.

2. Lewis, Tanya. (2014). Twins Separated at Birth Reveal Staggering Influence of Genetics. LiveScience. https://www.livescience.com/47288-twin-study-importance-of-genetics.html.

3. King's College London. (2012). *Psychopathy Linked to Brain Abnormalities.* Institute of Psychiatry, Psychology, and Neuroscience.

4. Hudson, Nathan, Roberts, Brent, & Lodi-Smith, Jennifer. (2012). *Personality Trait Development and Social Investment in Work.* Journal of research in Personality. Vol 46, Issue 3, pp. 334-344.

5. Marchione, Marilynn. (2018). *First Attempt to Permanently Change a Person's DNA to Cure a Disease Shows Promise.* USA Today. https://www.usatoday.com/story/news/2018/09/05/dna-study-gene-editing-hunter-syndrome-patients-shows-promise/1201738002/

6. Guerra, Julia. (2018). *Does Your Personality Change Over Time? You Are Who You Are, But Here's How You'll Grow.* https://www.elitedaily.com/p/does-your-personality-change-over-time-you-are-who-you-are-but-heres-how-youll-grow-10173733.

7. Booker, Karene. (2013). Scientists Discover How Brains Changes with Skills. Cornell Chronicle. http://news.cornell.edu/stories/2013/04/scientists-discover-how-brains-change-new-skills.

8. Harris, Judith Rich. (1998). *The Nurture Assumption: Why Children Turn Out the Way They Do.* The Free Press: Cortez, CO.

9. Dahhaj, Zaid. *12 Ways to Develop Self-Discipline.* Medium. https://medium.com/@zaiderrr/12-ways-to-develop-self-discipline-b59f9d57ca4f.

10. Martin, Steve J., Cialdini, Robert, & Goldstein, Noah. (2014). *The Small BIG.* Grand Central Publishing. **ISBN-13:** 978-1455584253

11. Morin, Amy. (2016). *How to Build Your Belief in Yourself.* Psychology Today. https://www.psychologytoday.com/us/blog/what-mentally-strong-people-dont-do/201610/how-build-your-belief-in-yourself.

12. Mavi, Michele. (n.d.) *10 Enviable Traits Disciplined People Have in Common.* FairyGodBoos. https://fairygodboss.com/articles/disciplined-people.

13. Cain, Aine. (2018). *A day in the life of Facebook CEO Mark Zuckerberg, who works up to 60 hours a week and has a squad of 12 employees to help him with social media.* Business Insider. https://www.businessinsider.com/mark-zuckerberg-daily-schedule-2017-6.

14. Noe, Alva. (2010). *Out of Our Heads: Why You are Not Your Brain and Other Lessons from the Biology of Consciousness.* Hill and Wang: New York City, New York.

15. Schein, Michael. (2010). *What Entrepreneurs Read (And It's Not What You Think).* Inc.com. https://www.inc.com/michael-schein/what-successful-entrepreneurs-read-it-s-not-what-you-think.html.

16. Waltron, Alice. (2015). *7 Ways Meditation Can Actually Train the Brain.* https://www.forbes.com/sites/alicegwalton/2015/02/09/7-ways-meditation-can-actually-change-the-brain/#54e7825b1465

17. Smith, Jacquelyn, & Gillett, Rachel. (2015). *18 Things Successful People Do in the First 10 Minutes of Their Work Day.* https://www.businessinsider.com/successful-people-do-these-things-in-the-first-10-minutes-at-work.

18. Gillett, Rachle. (2016). *How 19 Highly Successful People Stay in Shape.* Business Insider. https://www.businessinsider.com/exercise-routines-of-highly-successful-people-2016-4.

19. Kane, Colleen (2015). *The Fittest CEO in America?* Fortune. http://fortune.com/2015/05/05/fit-athletic-ceos/.

20. Godman, Heidi. *Regular Exercise Change the Brain to improve Memory, Thinking Skills.* Harvard Health Letter. https://www.health.harvard.edu/blog/regular-exercise-changes-brain-improve-memory-thinking-skills-201404097110

21. Gulec, Mustafa, et al. (2012). *Chronotype Effects on Psychopathology Levels in Healthy Young Adults.* Biological Rhythm Research. DOI: https://doi.org/10.1080/09291016.2012.704795

22. McGregor, Jena. (2015). *How 10 CEOs Work Smarter, Manage Better, and Get Things Done Faster.* Washington Post.

https://www.washingtonpost.com/news/on-leadership/wp/2015/01/02/how-10-ceos-work-smarter-manage-better-and-get-things-done-faster/?noredirect=on&utm_term=.9d778004f08f.

23. Willis, Judy. *The Neuroscience of Joyful Learning.* Engaging the Whole Child, Vol. 64, Summer 2007. https://www.psychologytoday.com/files/attachments/4141/the-neuroscience-joyful-education-judy-willis-md.pdf

24. Hughes, Bob. (2011). *Evolutionary Playwork.* Routledge. **ISBN-13:** 978-0415550857.

25. Beech, Stephen. *Slipped Up on Your New Year Diet? 'I Lost Ten Pounds By Cutting Myself Some Slack.'* 2016. Mirror. https://www.mirror.co.uk/news/real-life-stories/slipped-up-your-new-year-7118223.

26. Psychologist World. (2018). *Schemas and Memories.* https://www.psychologistworld.com/memory/schema-memory

27. Backman, Maurie. (2017). *The Science Behind Procrastination and How to Overcome It.* The Motley Fool. https://www.fool.com/careers/2017/12/11/the-science-behind-procrastination-and-how-to-over.aspx.

28. So, Timothy. (2017). *The Three Degrees of Influence and Happiness.* Positive Psychology News. https://positivepsychologynews.com/news/timothy-so/200911185246

29. Carter, Sherrie Bourg, Psy.D. (2012). *Why Mess Causes Stress: 8 Reasons, 8 Remedies.* Psychology Today. https://www.psychologytoday.com/us/blog/high-octane-women/201203/why-mess-causes-stress-8-reasons-8-remedies

30. Oxford Learning. (2017). *Is Multitasking Bad for Students?* https://www.oxfordlearning.com/multitasking-while-doing-homework-studying/.

31. Zeigarnik, Bluma Wolfuvna. (1965) *The Pathology of Thinking.* Moscow. **ASIN:** B0012SEPQ4.

32. Thoma, M., et al. (2013). *The Effect of Music on Human Stress Response.* PLOS One. Vol 8, Issue 8, DOI: [10.1371/journal.pone.0070156]

33. Shermer, Michael. (2008). *Patternicity: Finding Meaningful Patterns in Meaningless Noise.* Scientific American.

https://www.scientificamerican.com/article/patternicity-finding-meaningful-patterns/

34. Selig, Meg. (2017). *How Do Work Breaks Help Your Brain? 5 Surprising Answers.* Psychology Today.
https://www.psychologytoday.com/us/blog/changepower/201704/how-do-work-breaks-help-your-brain-5-surprising-answers.

35. Tottenham, Nim. PhD. Columbia University.

36. Hofman, S., Ph.D; Asnaani, Anu, M.A.; et al. *The Efficacy of Cognitive Behavioral Therapy.* Cognitive Therapy Res. 2012 Oct 1; 36(5): 427–440.
Published online 2012 Jul 31. DOI: [10.1007/s10608-012-9476-1]

37. Blatt, Rosemary. (1994). *The New American Workplace.* ILR Press.

38. Vandervilt, A., Oliveira, L., & Green, L. (2016). *Delay Dicounting - Pigeon, Rat, Human - Does it Matter?* J Exp Psychol Anim Learn Cogn. 2016 Apr; 42(2): 141–162.
Published online 2016 Feb 15. d: [10.1037/xan0000097]

39. Cowen, A. & Keltner, D. (2017). *Self-Report Captures 27 Distinct Categories of Emotion Bridged by Continuous Gradients.* PNS. https://doi.org/10.1073/pnas.1702247114.

40. Letswaart, M., Johnston, M., Dijkerman, H. C. , et al. *Mental Practice with Motor Imagery in Stroke Recovery: Randomized Controlled Trial of Efficacy.* Brain. 2011 May; 134(5): 1373–1386. Published online 2011 Apr 22. doi: [10.1093/brain/awr077]

41. Iso-Ahola, S. & Dotson, C. (2016). *Psychological Momentum – A Key to Continued Success.* Frontier Psychology. Vol 7, p. 1328. DOI: 10.3389/fpsyg.2016.01328

42. Ko, Ji & Strafella, A. (2012). *Dopaminergic Neurotransmission in the Human Brain: New Lessons from Perturbation and Imaging.* Neuroscientist. Vol 18, Issue 2, pp. 149-168. DOI: 10.1177/1073858411401413.

43. Burns, David. *Top 15 Cognitive Distortions.* http://www.pacwrc.pitt.edu/curriculum/313_MngngImpctTrmtcStrss ChldWlfrPrfssnl/hndts/HO15_ThnkngAbtThnkng.pdf

44. Moser, J., et al. (2017). *Third-Person Self-Talk facilitates emotion regulation without engaging cognitive control: Converging*

evidence from ERP and fMRI. Sci Rep. Vol 7, p. 4519.
doi: [10.1038/s41598-017-04047-3]

45. Leotti, L., Iyengar, S., & Ochsner, K. (2010). *Born to Choose: The Origins and Value for Need for Control.* Trends of Cognitive Science. Vol 14, Issue 10, pp. 457 – 463.
DOI: 10.1016/j.tics.2010.08.001

46. Goffman, Erving. (1956) *The Presentation of Self in Everyday Life.* Anchor. ISBN-13: 978-0385094023.

47. Skinner, B.F. (1976). *About Behaviorism.* Vintage Publishing. ISBN-13: 978-0394716183.

48. Duhigg, Charles. (2012). *The Power of Habit.* Random House Inc. *ISBN-13*: 978-0812981605

49. Piaget, Jean. (1896). *The Origins of Intelligence in Children.* Translated by Margaret Cook.
https://www.pitt.edu/~strauss/origins_r.pdf.

50. Kernbach, S., Eppler, M., & Bresciani, S. (2014). *The Use of Visualization in the Communication of Business Strategies.*

International Journal of Business Communication. Vol 52, Issue 2, pp. 2015. https://doi.org/10.1177/2329488414525444.

51. Simpson, E. & Balsam, P. (2016). *The Behavioral Neuroscience of Motivation: An Overview of Concepts, Measures, and Translational Applications.* Current Top Behavioral Neuroscience. Vol 27, pp. 1-2. DOI: [10.1007/7854_2015_402]

Daily Self-Discipline

Why You're Lacking Self-Discipline And 5 Ways To Develop It

By

Valentine Downey

Introduction

Most everyone would like to make some change in their life. All of us have an area in our life that we would like to improve upon. Perhaps the desired change involves our health, our relationships, or our finances. Whatever the desired change is, most people never see that change through completion. Many start with good intentions and try to change their life until they come across a source of resistance. When this happens, they often give up and return to our old habits.

Why is it that we so often give in to our weaknesses when we know that we would be happier if we made the change complete? The answer to this question is self-discipline. Having self-discipline is essential if we are going to make any significant change in our lives. Unfortunately, self-discipline is not a prevalent trait in our society. Seventy-five percent of Americans live paycheck to paycheck (Dickler, 2017). Approximately 75% of men and 60% of women are either overweight or obese (Murray, 2014). An estimated 60% of adults do not have a college degree (Mason, 2014). Even more surprising, only one in three Americans fulfilled with their lives (*Gregoire, 2013*).

Part of the challenge is that most of us lack an understanding of what is meant by self-discipline. What we do not understand that it is not enough to tell ourselves that we need to become self-disciplined. Just telling ourselves this is futile as it will not activate the motivation that we need to become self-disciplined. What is need is proven and scientifically based strategies that will allow you to move beyond the doldrums that keep you repeating your current behaviors and experience a breakthrough as you tap into your deeper potential.

In this book, I bring over 15 years of experience studying human potential, behavior modification, and neuro-linguistic programming. More importantly, I have successfully applied this knowledge to make changes in my own life. Before devoting my life to studying human potential, I was anything but self-disciplined. I had a passive personality, did not take risks, and I lacked any motivation to make any changes in my life, even though I was unhappy. For me, living with the known dullness of my life felt more comfortable than exerting myself and exposing myself to the unknown.

Today, no one who knows me would ever accuse me of not being self-disciplined. I hold three university degrees, work full-time as an educator, have a family, and I have a writing business. How I was in the past has become a faint memory.

The purpose of this book is to be your roadmap to self-discipline. The first part of the book will cover the principles behind science's understanding of self-discipline and the research. The second part of the book will provide you with powerful principles and strategies that will allow you to cultivate self-discipline with precision. All it takes is a desire to change your life and the willingness to do the work. This book will do the rest! One last special note: Also, the use of the words "self-discipline" and "willpower" are used interchangeably.

Chapter 1: The Fundamentals of Self-Discipline

There appears to be a fundamental law of life that allows it to operate effortlessly, an example of this would be the flight of a bird. When a bird flies, it encounters drag, which is created by the opposing force of the air as it moves forward. Rather than becoming a problem, the bird uses it to its benefit. The opposing force of the air flows underneath the bird's wings; thus, creating lift. The bird uses the resistance that it encounters to soar!

Rather than using resistance to our advantage, most of us avoid experiencing resistance. It is for this reason that most people have difficulty making changes in their lives. They give in to the resistance and go back to their old ways of doing things. Even if we know that our old habits are causing problems in our lives, at least we feel comfortable with them as we are familiar with that place. To overcome any resistance that we may encounter, we need to face the resistance and move forward until we break through. To do this requires self-discipline

.

What is Self-Discipline?

Self-discipline is a learned behavior; no one is born being self-disciplined. Like any other skill, self-discipline needs to be cultivated. It is the fruit that is yielded when we learn how to effectively challenge ourselves and experience the deeper inner potential that lies within us. Self-discipline is the ability to resist immediate gratification and be undeterred by the bumps on the road while moving toward what you are trying to achieve. In a survey by the American Psychological Association, the top reason given by respondents as to why they were not successful in making a change in their life was the lack of self-discipline or willpower. Twenty-seven percent of those who were surveyed reported that the lack of self-discipline was the greatest obstacle to making the life change they desired.

As for developing self-discipline, a common response to why they have not developed greater self-discipline was that their lives were too busy and that they did not have enough time to develop it. As we will explore later, this belief, along with many others, has not been supported by the research. Fortunately, what has proven to lead to the development of self-discipline is available to all of us.

Self-Discipline: A Misunderstood Power

One of the reasons why some of us may have adverse feelings toward developing self-discipline is the connotations that the term often carries with it. For many, the term "self-discipline" is associated with hard work, a lack of spontaneity, and being devoid of fun. In truth, self-discipline has less to do with the task that needs be done and more with developing our inner potential. Further, practicing self-discipline can become both a passionate and enjoyable pursuit. This is clearly seen when learning martial arts, a musical instrument, or being a scientist or an athlete.

Every person who has achieved greatness in their field of endeavor did what they loved or what they were good at. Because they love what they do, they invest themselves heavily in it. They are great at what they do because they devote their focus to it. When doing something you love, it is easy to miss the element of self-discipline that is involved. However, developing self-discipline for doing the things that we are not passionate about is more difficult.

Research is revealing that those who are self-discipline are not necessarily better at resisting temptations than those who are not self-disciplined. Rather, they avoid putting themselves in situations that would conflict with they are trying to achieve. As a result, they less frequently find themselves having to choose between short-term pleasure and long-term regret. In other words, people who have a high level of self-control have learned how to arrange their lives in a way that makes it easier to win in the game of life.

In the following chapters, you will learn powerful strategies to gain mastery over your mind and cultivate the self-discipline that will allow you to pursue your goals and become the person you want to be.

Benefits of Self-Discipline

There have been numerous researches on self-discipline, and all of the studies have arrived to the same conclusion: People who have self-discipline are happier with their life than those who have challenges with self-discipline. The University of Minnesota concluded that people who are self-disciplined were happier because they avoid placing themselves in situations that would conflict with problematic desires (American Psychological Association, n.d).

In a study by Duke University, researchers tracked the lives of 1,000 people from birth to age 32 as part of a health study. The results showed that those individuals who had a high level of self-control had greater mental and physical health at age 32 (American Psychological Association, n.d).

The study identified the participants with high self- control as children by feedback from their parents, teachers, and the participants themselves. Further, those participants who were identified as having high levels of self- control at an early age grew up to be adults who had a lower frequency of substance abuse or criminal convictions, saved more money, and enjoyed greater financial security. Also, the study controlled for other possible factors that may have influenced the results, such as socioeconomic status and intelligence (A PA, n.d).

Other studies revealed that students who had high levels of self-discipline had higher grades in school, better attendance records, and scored higher on standardized tests. The research shows that the level of self-control is a greater predictor of academic success than is the student's intelligence quotient (A PS, n.d).

The researchers went a step further by creating a scale that allowed them to score the level of self-discipline among the students who participated in the study. They found that there was a correlation between the level of the student's level of self-discipline with behaviors such as higher grade point averages, higher levels of self-esteem, and better relationship skills while less likely to engage in binge eating and alcohol abuse (Tian et al., 2018).

Hot and Cold: A Model to Understand Self-discipline

Around a decade ago, psychologist Walter Mischel ran an experiment to gain an understanding of self-discipline (American Psychological Association, n.d). His subjects were a group of preschoolers. One by one, Mischel tested each child by placing a plate in front of them that had a single marshmallow. He told the child that he needed the leave the room briefly. Before doing so, he told them that they had a choice. They could eat the marshmallow while he was gone, or they could hold off and not eat it. If they did the later, he would give them two marshmallows upon returning. Those children who did not eat the marshmallow were able to engage in delayed gratification. Their reward was that they got two marshmallows.

Overcoming the need for immediate gratification to enjoy a greater long-term reward is the essence of self-discipline. The only difference between the children in the study and the rest of us has to do with context. Instead of holding off from eating the marshmallow, it may mean not picking up a cigarette, though tempting, to live a healthier life. It may take the form of the decision not to go on a shopping spree and instead save that money for a more secure financial future. Maybe it involves resisting looking at our cell phone and give others are full attention so that they will feel appreciated.

Regardless of how it presents itself in our lives, we have a choice. We can take the easy way out and go with our impulses, or we can cultivate inner strength, allowing us to live a more fulfilling life and make a greater impact on others. As with any challenge that we may be facing, it is easier to overcome it if we first understand the challenge that we are facing. Based on Mischel's research, a model was developed to help understand how self-discipline functions (A PA, n.d).

Mischel refers to his model of self-discipline as a "hot and cold system." The "hot" component of the name refers to our cognitive nature. Simply stated, it is our rational thinking. It is our thoughts such:

- "Exercising will be good for my health."

- "I should not eat that food; it is fattening."

- "I need to stop smoking."

The "hot" component of the name refers to that aspect of us which is of an emotional or impulsive nature. When we exhibit self-discipline, we can resist becoming triggered by environmental factors such as cigarettes, alcohol, spending money, or eating. The "cold" part of the system is doing its job by reminding ourselves that resisting these things will lead to even more significant benefits later on.

When we do not exhibit self-discipline, the "hot" component kicks in. When giving in to this state of mind, we do not care if eating the proverbial marshmallow will mean missing out on getting two later on. We disregard the potential dangers of smoking and light up another one. We disregard the damage to our financial stability and purchase those items that we do not need. We consume the high-calorie food item, though our health is at risk.

When we do not practice self-discipline, we allow the world around us to become the master of our lives. We are but servants who willingly give in to impulses that are not in our best interest as we become triggered by those things which we desire.

Each one of us finds ourselves every day experiencing multiple situations where we can resist our temptations or give in to them.

Mischel followed up on the children of his experiment when they reached adolescence. What he discovered was remarkable. Most of the preschool children who were able to resist eating the marshmallow grew up to be successful in school as adolescents. They had higher standardized test scores, demonstrated a greater ability to plan, deal with stress, had greater coping skills when dealing with stressful situations, and showed a greater ability to concentrate without becoming distracted (APS, 2012).

Other experiments similar to Mischel's study were conducted and backed up his results. All the research found out that children who are self-disciplined retain their self-discipline into adulthood.

Self-Discipline: How Full is your Tank?

Many people who have trouble with self-discipline sincerely believe that they give into temptations because they are going through emotional events. An example of this is people who cheat on their diet because they are overwhelmed by an emotional experience. However, research does not support this. What researchers have discovered is that it is not the emotions that we experience that causes to lose our self-discipline but rather the depletion of willpower.

Later research on self-discipline built upon Mischel's findings and discovered another part of the puzzle as to why we lose our self-discipline and give into temptation. Researcher ran an experiment and discovered that resisting temptations can take its toll on us by depleting our self-discipline or willpower.

In one experiment, the participants of the study watched a movie with an emotional theme (A PA, n.d). Before watching the movie, the participants were divided into two groups. The first group was told to suppress their feelings while watching the movie while the second group was not given any special instructions. After the movie was over, the two groups were given a test involving physical stamina. The group that was told to suppress their emotions demonstrated less willpower during the test than the group that did not suppress their emotions when viewing the film.

Research by others supports this finding. Our self-discipline becomes depleted when we resist temptations after repeated exposure to it. When this happens, we are more likely to succumb to that which we are trying to resist (A PA, n.d). An example of this in real life is with those we refer to as "people pleasers," those who look to appease others. By trying to please other as the expense of their own feelings, "people pleasers" are more likely to deplete their willpower than those who deal with others on a genuine level by expressing how they feel.

Another example of this depletion of self-discipline is found when attempts to made to lose weight through dieting. The average person is bombarded by information from their environment about that which they are trying to avoid. A visit to the grocery store, commercials on television, social events, and fast food establishments are an ongoing source of triggers that the person who is trying to lose weight has to resist. For many, it is only a question of time when their depleted willpower gives way to giving in to their temptation. Losing self-discipline, due to depletion, is a natural occurrence in our self-discipline mechanism. Those who highly self-disciplined consciously, or unconsciously, know how to do prevent this from happening. Later in this book, you will learn secrets as to how to avoid this from happening.

A Self-Discipline Diet?

So far we have discussed how different factors influence self-discipline. We also discussed how self-discipline could be depleted through repetitively resisting temptations without reprieve. Now we will complicate things further. Researchers theorize that our blood sugar levels may play an important part in our ability to demonstrate self-discipline. They believe that when resisting temptations, our brains cells are actively working to maintain self-control.

The brain is a high energy consumption organ that is fueled by glucose. Some researchers theorize that self-discipline depletion is the result of an overworked brain. However, as with other research on self-discipline, this theory has been challenged.

Other studies have concluded that there is a mechanism that overrides the drop in glucose as some subjects in experiments were able to demonstrate self-discipline even at low glucose levels. Some argue that the mechanism that can override low glucose levels is beliefs, the topic of the next section (American Psychological Association, n.d).

The Power of Belief and Motivation

We have just explored a number of factors that can affect self-discipline. We discussed how self-discipline is the ability to resist immediate gratification to achieve a greater long-term goal. We also discussed how our ability to resist immediate gratification could be depleted if our resistance is repeatedly tested without the opportunity for reprieve.

New research is showing that our understanding of the depletion of self-discipline is far from being complete. If your car is low in gas, the only way to fill your tank is to add more gas. Research is now showing that depleted self-discipline can be restored just by changing what you believe!

The idea that self-discipline can be depleted would seem to apply that it is a limited resource. However, this idea was blown out of the water as the result of a 2010 Stanford University study (Tian, et al., 2018). They discovered that participants who believed willpower was a limited resource experienced self-discipline depletion. Other participants did not believe that willpower was a limited resource. These individuals did not experience self-discipline depletion after being exposed to conditions that usually would cause it.

The idea that there is a limited amount of self-discipline was also challenged in an experiment that tested the effects of motivation. In the experiment; participants were given a task to do after their self-discipline was depleted. One group performed at a lower level on the task as compared to when the task was performed when their self-discipline was not depleted. The other group was told that they would be paid for doing the task. Despite, having depleted willpower, this group found the motivation to perform the task and completed it successfully (Tian et al., 2018).

Motivation: The Question of Pursuit or Retreat

Self-discipline is the fruit that grows from motivation and an empowered belief system. What sustains self-discipline is motivation. In turn, motivation is created by our desire to move toward that which makes us feel good or by our desire to move away from that which we want to avoid.

Based on this, we can say that self-discipline is the fruit of the motivation that occurs when we pursue what we perceive will lead to pleasure or avoid what we perceive will lead to feeling pain. Notice the key word here is "perceive." Exercising is good for us, but we will not exercise if we perceive that it will lead to unpleasant experiences. Conversely, smoking is proven to be dangerous to your health; however, many people smoke despite this. Why, because they perceive smoking to be pleasurable.

The interpretation that we have of whether something is pleasurable or aversive is found our beliefs. There is no inherent meaning in anything in life. The mind creates all meaning.

To develop self-discipline, we need to be motivated. To be motivated, we need to learn how to manage our beliefs. If we do not learn to take charge of our beliefs, we may succumb to procrastination, which is not doing something we should be doing because of the unpleasant feelings that we associate with it. Self-discipline involves overriding the negative associations that we have for the task that needs to be done. When we can manage our beliefs, we take charge of the meaning that we give to our experiences.

Imagine a teenager who loves to party but grudgingly does his school work. The parents of the teenager may have concerns about his attitude toward school and tell him that he needs to practice self-discipline. The problem with his parents just telling him that he needs to practice self-discipline is that it ignores the motivation component that sustains self-discipline. The teenager may buckle down for a while to appease his parents; however, he will do so without having the motivation to back him up. Because of this, he will most likely drift back to his patterns of behavior.

The reason why he feels motivated to party goes back to what we previously discussed, that we are motivated to pursue what we perceive will lead to pleasurable experiences while avoiding that which we feel will result in unpleasant experiences. These associations are what are commonly known as "beliefs."

The teenager has beliefs where he associates partying with pleasure and studying with unpleasant feelings. If the parents want to get their son to change his behavior, they need to stop telling him to practice self-discipline and help him change his beliefs about partying and homework. In other words, they need to help him associate pleasurable feelings with studying and unpleasant feelings with his frequent partying.

Changing our behavior requires changing our beliefs, the meaning that we attribute to our experience. Maybe the teenager finds out that he is flunking and dreads what his parents will say if they find out. Suddenly, he associates bringing up his grades with pleasure (or the avoiding of pain) and partying with pain. Because he becomes motivated to study, he resists the temptations of partying and other distractions while maintaining his focus on studying.

While motivation is a significant factor demonstrating self-discipline, the kind of motivation exhibited is an important consideration. In a research experiment, participants were given a plate of cookies, which they were told not to eat. After resisting eating the cookies, the participants were given a task to complete that involved physical exertion. What they found is that the participants who did not eat the cookies out of an internal motive outperformed the participants who did not eat the cookies out of external motives (APA, n.d).

So what does this mean? Internal motives are motives that are based on how we feel; they are based upon our desires. An example of an internal motive is not eating the cookies because you want to lose weight. The desire to remain on a diet is driven by the inner desire to achieve weight loss or greater health. External motivation is based on gaining the approval of others. While the person may want to eat the cookies, they do not eat them out of the desire to please the researcher.

No One is Left Out

Regardless of what we may believe about ourselves, no one is left out of the many benefits that come with developing self-discipline. Self-discipline is an inherent potential that exists within us all. We can think of self-discipline as a muscle. If we do not exercise a muscle, it becomes weak and atrophies. If we go to the gym and exercise the muscle, it will become stronger. However, building muscles are done over time with consistent workouts. To build muscle, it first must be broken down.

When working out, the muscle becomes fatigued and breaks down. During the rest period between workouts, the muscle not only regains energy but becomes stronger. Self-discipline is like a muscle, the more you exercise it, the stronger it becomes. Eventually, being self-disciplined becomes a habit, a habit that becomes rewarding within itself. For this reason, less motivation is needed to sustain it; it becomes part of whom the person is.

Chapter 2: Your Self-Discipline Work Out

Up to now, you have received a lot of information about self-discipline. You probably also noticed that a lot of the information seemed too inconclusive, contradictory, or just complicated. Do not worry about this. This information was provided to give you background information on what is known about self- discipline and the theories that were derived from that information. The value of this information is that it provides context for the strategies and exercises that are found in the next section.

Before going any further, I need to make an important statement. I know that some of you are thinking that you are not interested in finishing this book or doing the exercises. You may rationalize that you know everything that you already know everything that you read so far. Perhaps you're thinking that doing that the exercises will be too much work or that you do not have the time. You picked up this book for a reason, which is that you want to make a change in your life. Let me also remind you of the statistics that were given earlier in the book:

- Seventy-five percent of Americans live paycheck to paycheck.

- Approximately 75% of men and 60% of women are either overweight or obese.

- An estimated 60% of adults do not have a college degree.

- Only one in three Americans feel are excited or fulfilled with their lives.

The question that you need to ask yourself is do you want to live like most of the population, or do you want to live a life that is exceptional, a life where you feel in charge, and you are shaping your future. We discussed earlier that the forces of pain and pleasure are what motivates us to take action. I invite you to do the following exercise (Robbins, 1992) to shore up your commitment that you will do the exercises in this book.

Do the following:

1. Get three sheets of paper. Select a paper size of 8" x 11" or larger.

2. On the first sheet, write down as many beliefs that you have as to why you do not have the self-discipline that you would like. Examples are:

   - There is nothing that I can do about it.

   - Becoming self-disciplined is too hard.

   - Being self-disciplined will take the fun out of life.

   - I made attempts to change in the past but have always failed.

3. When writing this list, it is important to write as fast as possible without taking time to think about it. Write down whatever comes to you. Doing the exercise in this manner

will help you access deeper levels of your awareness as you will less likely get caught up in your mind.

4. When finished, review your list and select the top three reasons for what has prevented you from becoming self-disciplined.

5. From your short list, pick the top reason that you believe has prevented you from reaching your goal.

6. Take a second sheet and fold it in half lengthwise.

7. On the top of the paper, write down the belief that you selected.

8. After writing down your belief, make a list on the left-hand side of the paper of all the ways that holding this belief has cost you in your life. Ask yourself how this belief has impacted you emotionally, your self-esteem, your health, your relationships, and your finances.

9. When writing this list, do the following:

   a. Write down the first thing that comes to your mind, even if it seems irrelevant.

   b. Write as fast as you can and feel the emotions that arise. This is a heartfelt exercise, not a cerebral one.

   c. Keep writing until you cannot think of what to write.

10. By each item, you write down, assign an arbitrary point value as to how much weight this item has had on you.

When selecting the point value, choose the first number that comes to mind.

11. When you have completed assigning the point values, find the total of all the point values and place it at the bottom of the page.

12. For the right side of the page, repeat steps 8-11, except this time you will write down all the ways that this belief has benefited you.

13. On the second paper, write a new alternative belief which supports you. For example, if the belief you had on the first paper was "Changing is too difficult," your new belief could be "Changing is difficult but it will be worth it."

14. Repeat Steps 7-12, though this time you will do the Steps 8 and 12 in reverse. In other words, write down all the ways that you would believe that you would benefit from this new belief when doing Step 8 and write down all the ways your new belief would cost you in Step 12.

15. When you have completed the two sheets, do the following:

    a. Immediately review your lists, allowing yourself to experience any emotions that arise fully.

    b. Review your lists every day, once in the morning and once before you go to bed until you become fully associated with the emotions that you experience.

By becoming fully with associated the feelings that you experience when you think of the costs of your old beliefs and the benefits that you would obtain from adopting your new ones, your mind will become reprogrammed with your new belief (Robbins, 1992). Now that you have gained leverage on your self, it is time to work out and develop your self-discipline!

Chapter 3: Level 1 Exercises

Level 1 Exercises are fundamental exercise or strategies that will allow you to focus directly on starting the process of cultivating self-discipline. We will start with goal setting and then move your belief system.

Whatever we focus on in life becomes our reality. At the most basic level, the reasons why people do not accomplish their goals is because they do not have a structure to follow, which often leads us to become distracted. The power of goal setting is that it causes you to focus on what you want to achieve.

Goal Setting

The most common mistakes when goal setting includes:

- Goals that are too general.
- Having goals that are not measurable.
- Creating goals without a time frame or due date.

The following procedure departs from the traditional approach to goal setting addresses all these concerns while offering the opportunity to discover where your passions and creating a well-rounded life. The following are the steps to use this innovative method of goal setting. We will start with your personal goals:

Step 1: Brainstorm

Get a piece of paper and start writing down whatever you would like to accomplish in your personal life. When doing this, it is important to write rapidly. Don't take time to think about; write down whatever comes to mind. Do not worry about spelling or specifics. This list is just meant to get out on paper what you have wished for in your heart. As with the previous exercises on belief changes, it is important to keep writing until you cannot write anymore. When thinking of your personal, consider things like:

- What would you like to improve in your life?

- What would you like to learn or discover?

- What would you like to achieve or experience?

- What qualities of yourself would you like to develop further?

Step 2: After making your list, go over each item and give it a timeline of when you want to accomplish that goal. Choose one of the following: 1 year or less, two years or less, or 3 years or less. For longer-term goals, you can use time frames such as for ten years or less, 20 years or less, and so on.

Next, choose your top 1-year personal goal and write about it. When you are writing about it, you want to paint an image in your mind that will excite you. Include the following information:

- Why you are committed to achieving this goal.

- How will you benefit upon achieving your goal.

- What the impact to you will be if you do not achieve your goal.

Step 3: When you are finished repeat the same process of the following areas in your life:

- Financial: What goals would you like to accomplish in your work or finances?

- Contribution Goals: What goals would you like to accomplish that result in contributing to others?

- Thing Goals: What would you like to obtain or what kind of adventure would you like to experience. Is there something you always wanted to buy or a certain place that you have always wanted to travel to?

When you have finished these steps, you will have your top three goals for the year that include your personal life, your finances, contribution, and for fun or personal enrichment. The following are some additional points to consider when goal setting:

- **Goals Setting is a Practice in Self-Discipline**

Research has demonstrated that setting goals increased self-discipline as it causes us to focus our attention on what we want to achieve. Consider the following when setting goals:

- **Make Your Goals Challenging but Realistic**
  The link between motivation and developing self-discipline is strong (APS, 2012). If you lose your motivation to achieve your goals, you will most likely return to your old habits.

  For this reason, the goals that you set should seem challenging to you while at the same being achievable. Also, try breaking down your goals down into baby steps. In doing this, you will gain confidence with each baby step that you take.

- **Make Yourself Accountable**
  Research has shown that people who have challenges with self-discipline view those who are disciplined in a favorable matter. When you have created your goals, share them with someone whom you respect. Doing this will give you greater motivation to accomplish your goals.

Planning

Now that you have established your goals, here are some things to consider when you create your plans for how you are going to achieve your goals:

1. Start with the end in mind

2. Envision in your mind what it would like if your goals were your reality today! If you were experiencing your goals at this moment, what would you see? What would you hear? What would you feel? What would you taste? Use questions like these to make your goals come alive.

3. With the vision of your goals in your mind, work backward by thinking of all the things that would have to happen for you to achieve your goal. Write them down as you keep your vision of your goal fresh in your mind.

4. When you have a list of activities that need to be accomplished, turn each item on the list into an action item. Commit yourself that you will accomplish this item by a specific date. Some items on your list will require multiple action items for it to be accomplished. Example: If one of the things that you need to do is take a course or get training, your action items may be:

   a. Research schools in my area

   b. Visit the schools that I believe will fit my needs.

   c. Inquire on financial assistance.

   d. Enroll in the school.

For tasks with multiple action items, rank them according to priority and then schedule a date for when you are committed to accomplishing each action item.

Implementation Intention

A term used for a technique used by psychologist, implementation intention refers to the creating of a plan for when you encounter challenges while working toward your goals. An example would be a person whose goal is to quit smoking. At some point, the desire to smoke will take hold of them. The person would develop a plan for what they will do when they desire a cigarette, which may include taking a walk or call a friend.

Rewarding Yourself

Make sure to you reward yourself each time you move closer to your goals. Doing so will motivate you to repeat your actions in the future. With enough repetition, your actions will become winning habits.

When you have developed your goals and your plan for achieving them, the next step is to look at your beliefs. The beliefs that you hold will either propel you toward your goal's achievement, or they will result in you giving up before you even started.

Mastering Your Beliefs

Beliefs are a form of thought of which we have a sense of certainty about; thus, they have a greater impact on us than thoughts do. The thought "I want ice cream" is unstable in that it can enter your mind one moment but leave seconds later if your attention becomes occupied by something else. The belief "I am undisciplined" is more resilient than the thought of ice cream. To change a belief requires a willingness to be open to an alternative perspective, which is what this section's exercise will demonstrate.

Our beliefs are very powerful, so powerful that they drive every aspect of our lives. Our beliefs determine what we focus on, what we overlook, what we are willing to do, what we will avoid, our relationship with others, and how we experience the world. We can think of our beliefs as tinted sunglasses. If you are wearing sunglasses that are tinted blue, everything that you experience will appear to be blue. If a person believes that they are undesirable because of their weight, that belief will determine what that person focus on, what they are oblivious of, who they associate with, how they live their life, and how they perceive others and themselves.

Just as with thoughts, beliefs lack any inherent power of their own; our beliefs are energized by the amount of attention that we give them. Your beliefs rely on you to obtain their power. Further, your beliefs are neither true nor false, nor do they reflect true reality. Rather, our beliefs create our reality!

In 1954, the world speed record for running a mile was broken by Roger Bannister, who ran a mile in less than four minutes. Before Bannister, no runner had ever run a mile under four minutes. Since Bannister's record achievement, many other runners have run a mile under four minutes, so many in fact that Bannister's running time became a new standard for other runners.

Why is it that no runner completed the mile run in less than four minutes before Bannister's achievement? Why is it that so many runners have beaten Bannister's record since then? The answer to these questions is the power of belief. Bannister's achievement showed other runners what was possible. Until Bannister, it was believed that running a mile in less than four minutes was not possible.

Our beliefs are a demonstration of the Law of Attraction working. When we energize a thought by focusing our awareness on it, that thought attracts other thoughts of like quality, just as a magnet attracts iron filings. A person may have the thought "I am overweight." By repeatedly giving this thought their attention, this thought becomes energized and starts to attract other thoughts such as:

- "I need to diet."

- "I am unattractive."

- "I am a pig."

- "I need to lose weight."

- "I have always failed to lose weight."

- "Diets never work."

Any thought that is attracted to the original thought "I am overweight" becomes the potential target of our attention. If this occurs, it will also become energized and attract other thoughts like "I guess, I was born this way" or "I need to join a health club." It is this process that creates a belief. In the following exercise, you will identify your disempowering beliefs that are preventing you from achieving the goal that you desire to achieve.

Belief Balance Sheet

This exercise (Robbins, 1992) is designed to replace your limiting beliefs with empowering ones. The exercise has two parts, and you will need three sheets of paper.

Part 1

1. Think about the times that you have set goals in the past but never saw them to fruition. List them on the first sheet of paper.

2. As you think about those instances, ask yourself why you did not accomplish your goals. Write them down.

3. Review your reasons for not accomplishing your goals. Do you see a pattern? What is it? Write it down.

4. When you have identified the reason(s), determine what belief do you have about yourself that underlies your reasons. Anytime we give a reason for not doing something, we are revealing a belief that we have about ourselves. Remember we move toward situations that we perceive will provide pleasure and avoid those that we perceive will lead to pain. What is the painful feeling that you were trying to avoid? Were you afraid of failure? Were you afraid of what others would think? Were you afraid of succeeding?

5. Take the second sheet and fold it in half lengthwise.

6. On top of the paper, write down the limiting belief.

7. After writing down your belief, make a list on the left-hand side of the paper of all the ways that holding this belief has cost you in your life. When writing, keep in mind the following:

   a. When writing this list, write down the first thing that comes to your mind, even if it seems irrelevant.

   b. Write as fast as you can and feel the emotions that arise. This is a heartfelt exercise, not a cerebral one.

   c. Keep writing until you cannot think of what to write.

8. By each item, you write down, assign an arbitrary point value as to how much weight this item has had on you. When selecting the point value, choose the first number that comes to mind.

9. When you have completed assigning the point values, find the total of all the point values and place it at the bottom of the page.

10. For the right side of the page, repeat steps 7-9, except this time you will write down all the ways that this belief has benefited you.

Part 2

1. Come up with a new empowering belief to replace the limiting belief that you used at the beginning of this exercise. For example, if the belief you had on the first paper was "I am afraid of failing," your more empowering belief may be "Fearing failure is normal, and I will not let that stop me."

2. Take the third sheet and fold it in half lengthwise.

3. On top of the paper, write down your new empowering belief.

4. After writing down your belief, make a list on the left-hand side of the paper of all the ways that you think your new belief would benefit you. When writing, keep in mind the following:

   a. When writing this list, write down the first thing that comes to your mind, even if it seems irrelevant.

b. Write as fast as you can and feel the emotions that arise. This is a heartfelt exercise, not a cerebral one.

c. Keep writing until you cannot think of what to write.

5. By each item, you write down, assign an arbitrary point value as to how much weight this item has had on you. When selecting the point value, choose the first number that comes to mind.

6. When you have completed assigning the point values, find the total of all the point values and place it at the bottom of the page.

7. For the right side of the page, repeat Steps 4-6, except this time you will write down all the ways your new belief will cost you.

When you have completed the two sheets, do the following:

1. Immediately review your lists, allowing yourself to experience any emotions that arise fully.

2. Review your lists every day, once in the morning and once before you go to bed until you become fully associated with the emotions that you experience.

By becoming fully with associated the feelings that you experience when you think of the costs of your old beliefs and the benefits that you would obtain from adopting your new ones, your mind will become reprogrammed with your new belief (Robbins, 1992).

Having completed this exercise, you have taken a major step in growing your self-discipline. Your beliefs are so powerful that they determine your behavior and what you believe is possible.

The next section deals with a function of your psychology that is just as powerful as your beliefs, which are your values.

Your Value System

We often associate values with things like family, country, or friendship. This view reflects our societal conditioning which leads to a dualistic perspective. From this perspective, we see ourselves as separate entities from the world around us. We identify people, places, and things as what we value.

This book takes a different approach, one which is used neurolinguistic programming (NLP). NLP is the study of how we organize our thinking, language, feelings, and behavior in order to achieve a specific outcome.

From the NLP perspective, values are not things that exist outside ourselves; rather, they are the feelings that we want to experience. To better understand this, consider the following example:

Let us say that I ask you what you value, and you reply by saying that you value family. I would then ask you "What does family give you?" You respond by saying that family gives you a sense of belonging. Because the sense of belonging is what you really value; family is just a means that you use to experience a sense of belonging.

Similarly, someone may say that they value money. If you inquire to what money would give them, they may come up with responses such as "power" or "security." As with "belonging," "power" and "security" are states of feeling. How things make us feel is what we ultimately value. Family or money is just the means by which we experience these feelings, but they are not their source. All feeling and emotional states are generated from within us. It is our conditioning and our identifying with the physical realm that leads us to fall for the illusion that our emotional needs are dependent upon something outside ourselves.

For the first part of this exercise (Robbins, 1992) do the following:

1. Make a list of all the things that you value (For this step, just list what comes to mind. Do not worry about getting into the emotional states that they seem to offer.

2. By each item on your list, ask yourself "What does_____give me?" or "What would I get from having___?

3. Whatever response you get, keep asking the question until you identify the emotional state. Here is an example:

   a. I value my truck.

   b. What does my truck give me? Answer: The ability to drive where I want, regardless of the terrain.

   c. What does the ability to drive in any terrain give me? Answer: Freedom

   d. Freedom is an emotional state and thus is the final answer.

4. After you have made the list of emotional states that you value, your next step is to place them in a hierarchy. Think about which emotional state you value the most. Which emotional state comes second in its level of importance to you? The easiest way is to ask the question "If I could only choose one emotional state, which one would I not be willing to live without?"

5. When you have identified that emotional state, you would repeat this question with the remaining emotional states on your list until you have identified the hierarchy of each emotion.

6. With each emotional state that you have in your hierarchy, ask yourself what you could think or do in order to experience that emotional state. By doing this, you no longer have to rely on something outside of yourself to experience these emotional states. Instead, you will be in

full control whenever you want to experience that emotional state.

Here is an example:

a. I value family.

b. I have learned that what I really value is a sense of belonging.

c. Knowing this, I can think of all the ways that I can experience the emotional state of belonging, even when my family is not around. Examples could be:

    i. Taking the time to think about why I love my family.

    ii. Thinking about what I could do to create happiness for others.

    iii. Joining an organization that is devoted to a goal that is important to me.

By doing this exercise, you will know the emotional states that you value and how to experience them without having to depend on something outside yourself.

Another value for doing this exercise is that it will allow you to see if you have conflicting values. The source of all interpersonal and inner conflict is a conflict in values. Imagine that in your value hierarchy you have two conflicting values: independence and connection. You value your independence yet you want to be in a relationship.

Understanding how you can experience the emotional states associated with these two values will allow you to resolve the conflict. Perhaps, after some reflection, you realize that being assertive and communicating your needs to your partner will allow you to enjoy the emotional state of independence while at the same time being in a relationship (Robbins, 1992).

Doing the previous exercises may lead you to develop insights about yourself that you previously may have not been aware of. Keeping a journal is a great way to record your insights, your hopes and fears, and developing greater clarity of your experiences. It is also an exercise in self-discipline.

Chapter 4: Level 2 Exercises

Long Term Success: Developing Self-Discipline through Contribution

In the previous sections, you did exercises to clarify your beliefs and create new empowering ones. You also examined your values, which determine what we move toward and what we avoid. With this insight, you are ready now to use what you learn and direct toward developing new habits, based on self-discipline, that will allow you to move forward to achieve your goals as well as clarification of what is it that you really want from life. You will start with the power of contribution.

The Power of Contribution

The fundamental reason why we experience problems with self-discipline goes back to the twin forces of pain and pleasure. We gravitate toward that which we perceive will result in pleasurable experiences and avoid those situations that we perceive will result in us experiencing painful experiences.

We have learned to avoid demonstrating self-discipline as a way to justify ourselves not putting ourselves in a position where we may fail and look bad. After all, failing in an endeavor might lead to us being judged by others. The fear of being judged comes from ego-based thinking. If we listen to the voice of our ego-based thoughts, it is giving us the following message: *It is safer to be undisciplined than it is to caught trying to pursue a worthy goal and fall short.*

With the understanding that it is our ego that keeping us from demonstrating self-discipline, it is easy to understand why contribution is such a powerful force for overcoming the games that our minds play on us. There is a reason why all religions stress the importance of contribution. There is a reason why offenders in the criminal justice system are often ordered to perform community service. There is a reason why most people who volunteer their time love doing so. What is the reason? It is because contributing to others gives a sense of meaning to our lives.

There is nothing that elevates our experience of life more than impacting the lives of others. Contribution, when done from the heart, gives a sense of meaning to our lives. A matter of fact, you will learn in Chapter Six that contribution is one of our six human needs. As humans, we have a need to be able to contribute in order to experience fulfilment in our lives.

The power of contribution is easy to understand if we take time to reflect on our own lives. Is'nt true that you are willing to do more for those that you love than you would do for yourself? The power of contribution is that it causes us to shift the focus of our attention from ourselves and place it on others. When you remove your focus off from yourself and place it on others, you free yourself from your ego.

There are innumerable ways that you can contribute to others. If you have trouble coming up with ideas, ask yourself how you can create values for others. For this chapter, contribution is not donating money. To develop self-discipline, you want to give of yourself.

If you have challenges with self-discipline, you may be resistant to contributing. If this is true, it is important to remind yourself what was discussed earlier: All behavior is governed by the forces of pain and pleasure. If you believe you are undisciplined, it is because you have associated less pain with being undisciplined than with being disciplined. Or, you associate greater happiness with being undisciplined than you do with being disciplined.

If you have not done so already, I recommend that you do the exercise in Chapter 2. If you have done this exercise, the following is a way to align your love and passions with contributing to others. Doing the following exercises will let you develop greater clarity to what drives you and how you can use that to benefit others.

Exercise: Discovering what brings you Happiness

In this exercise, think of times when you were the happiest and record them in a journal. When writing, consider the following:

- What were you doing at the time?

- Where were you when you were doing it?

- Who were you with?

Record as many memories as possible, doing this will help you see patterns in your life for when you were the happiest. These patterns will play an important role in understanding your purpose in life.

Exercise: Identifying Your Strength or Talents

In this exercise, you will reflect on your strengths and talents. People often have trouble identifying their strengths or talents as they may be subtle and not obvious to them. Being patient with others, being caring of others, standing up for justice, a sense of humor, having a high degree of tolerance, artistic abilities, communication skills, being compassionate, being self- reflective, noticing how things relate to each other, noticing how things do not relate to each other, all of these are examples of potential strengths and talents. The following are prompts to help you in your thinking:

- Is there something about you that you are frequently complimented on?

- Is there something that you do that seems effortless to you?

- Is there some activity that you engage in which causes you to lose all track of time?

List your qualities that others admire or the activities that are effortless for you or cause you to lose all sense of time.

Exercise: Identifying Needs

In this exercise, you are going to focus on those around you and discover what needs are not being met. Focus on individuals, members of your family, your friends, neighbors, those that you work with, your employer, and those that you do not know. Focus on your own home, your neighborhood, and your community. Ask yourself "What needs are not being met?" or "How could I create greater value for those around me?"

When you have found needs that are not being met, reflect on ways that you can utilize your strengths or talents in addressing these needs.

The following is a journaling exercise that you can use that incorporates the elements of finding your purpose.

Exercise: Journaling

1. In your journal, do the following:

2. Make a list of all the things that you enjoy doing.

3. Make a list of your skills, talents, and that which you are knowledgeable about.

4. Make a list of all the needs that you are aware of that are being experienced by your family, community, state, or country.

5. Reflect on how you can integrate Steps 1-3 into serving those you indicated in Step 4.

For example, someone may identify relationship skills, artistic ability, and marketing as their strengths. They also may have identified neighborhood blight as a problem in their community. This person could serve their neighborhood by organizing a group of people to beautify their neighborhood by removing graffiti and creating murals and forms of artwork for people to enjoy. Using their knowledge of marketing, they would be able to create partnerships with the business community for the purpose of acquiring needed resources.

It is true that you could not bother doing this exercise and find a way to serve others. The advantage of doing this exercise is that by aligning you gifts and abilities. You will be able to create even greater impact on those you are serving as well as for yourself.

Here are some additional suggestions:

- Write in your journal everything that comes to your mind, even if it does not seem to make sense or seems unimportant. Don't' think about it, write as fast as you can without stopping. Keep writing until you cannot come up with any more ideas.

- The key to this exercise is to look deeply into the world around you. Do not get fooled by thoughts like "There is no need," or "Things are so bad that I cannot make a difference." These are just excuses that your ego is making. There is always a need to be met.

Continue to reflect on this exercise to deepen your understanding of how you can contribute to others. Those who contribute to others often indicate that they were the ones that benefitted the most from the experience. They report that their lives are richer and more fulfilled.

As you will discover in Chapter 6, to contribute to others meets an inherent need that exists within us all. Without contributing to others, we are unable to experience fulfilled lives. When we contribute to others, we learn more about ourselves. We gain a greater sense of identity, which is the topic of the next section.

Chapter 5: Level 3 Exercises

Questioning Your Beliefs about Yourself

Your sense of identity is crucial in discovering your life purpose because your sense of identity determines what you are willing or not willing to do. You did not consciously choose your beliefs, nor did you consciously choose your sense of identity. These things became part of your conditioning as a member of society. To find your life's purpose, you need to reevaluate your sense of identity and determine if it is helping you access your life's purpose.

Creating Your New Identity

When we change the beliefs that we have of ourselves, we change an aspect of our identity. To access our purpose of life, we want to foster those beliefs about ourselves that allow the authentic expression of who we are. A person who has hidden potential to be a great actor will never realize it if that person's beliefs about themselves prevent them from experiencing those situations that draw out that potential. If this person has the belief that appearing before an audience would be terrifying, that belief will prevent this person from ever realizing their potential.

If this person changes their beliefs that appearing in front of an audience, even if they make mistakes, would not be the end of the world, that person will allow him or herself to take the risk and experience their hidden potential. The experience of being on stage in front of an audience will elicit their hidden potential to express itself. It will feel right to this person, even if they screw up. There will be a sense from within this person that "This is what I was meant to do! This is what I have been looking for!"

As stated before, your sense of identity is just a group of beliefs that you have bought into. Because we believe these beliefs to be who we are, what we think and how we behave reflects those beliefs. In previous exercises, you identified limiting beliefs about yourself and then identified how they have negatively impacted your life. You then replaced those limiting beliefs with empowering ones. You also identified all the benefits of having that belief. In this exercise, you will do the same thing exercise to develop a sense of identity that will improve your alignment with your purpose.

Exercise: Changing Your Identity

This exercise has two parts and requires three sheets of a paper:

Part 1

1. Ask yourself how you want to be as a person. What would you have to believe about yourself to feel happy and live the life that you desire? When an answer comes to you, write it down.

2. Repeat the question to yourself again. Again, write down the first thing that comes to your mind. Keep doing this until you have created a list. Here are some examples:

- I want to be more assertive.

- I want to take more risks.

- I do not want to be afraid of making mistakes.

- I want to be more outgoing.

3. Take the third sheet and fold it in half lengthwise.

4. Using your list, rank each item in order of priority as to how important it is to you.

5. On top of the paper, write down your top item. For example, I want to be more assertive.

6. After writing down your belief, make a list on the left-hand side of the paper of all the ways that not being assertive has cost you in your life. When writing, keep in mind the following:

   a. When writing this list, write down the first thing that comes to your mind, even if it seems irrelevant.

   b. Write as fast as you can and feel the emotions that arise. This is a heartfelt exercise, not a cerebral one.

   c. Keep writing until you cannot think of what to write.

7. By each item you write down, assign an arbitrary point value as to how much weight this item has had on you. When selecting the point value, choose the first number that comes to mind.

8. When you have completed assigning the point values, find the total of all the point values and place it at the bottom of the page.

9. For the right side of the page, repeat Steps 5-7, except this time you will write down all the ways that you have benefited from not being assertive.

Part 2

1. Take the third sheet and fold it in half lengthwise.

2. Take your top item for the list and turn it into an empowering belief about yourself. For example, if your top item was "*I want to be more assertive*," change it to "*I am becoming more assertive.*"

3. Write your new belief on top of the paper.

4. After writing down your belief, make a list on the left-hand side of the paper of all the ways that you think that your new belief would benefit you in your life. When writing, keep in mind the following:

   • Write down the first thing that comes to your mind, even if it seems irrelevant.

- Write as fast as you can and feel the emotions that arise. This is a heartfelt exercise, not a cerebral one.

- Keep writing until you cannot think of what to write.

5. By each item you write down, assign an arbitrary point value as to how much weight this item has had on you. When selecting the point value, choose the first number that comes to mind.

6. When you have completed assigning the point values, find the total of all the point values and place it at the bottom of the page.

7. For the right side of the page, repeat steps 4-6, except this time you will write down all the ways that your new belief may cost you.

8. By each item you write down, assign an arbitrary point value as to how much weight this item has had on you. When selecting the point value, choose the first number that comes to mind.

9. When you have completed assigning the point values, find the total of all the point values and place it at the bottom of the page.

10. When you are done, review your lists and compare the point totals. For your new belief, how does the point total for the benefits compare with that of the costs?

When you have completed the two sheets, do the following:

- Immediately review your lists, allowing yourself to fully experience any emotions that arise.

- Review your lists every day, once in the morning and once before you go to bed until you become fully associated with the emotions that you experience.

- By becoming fully with associated the feelings that you experience when you think of the costs of your old beliefs and the benefits that you would obtain from adopting your new ones, your mind will become reprogrammed with your new belief.

Chapter 6: Level 4 Exercises

Expanding Your Sense of Identity

Now that you have identified the way you want to be, and you have become clear of the benefits of being that way, it is time to instill that new quality in your life. There are two ways of doing it: The first method is more simple but does not leave more room for problems to occur. The second method is more complex but offers greater precision in making a change in behavior.

Be It until you are It

Little kids with their imagination often pretend to be a superhero during play. They get so into it during these moments that they become them. A good actor will study his character's mannerisms, belief systems, and idiosyncrasies and adopt them as his own as he prepares for the part. Both of these scenarios are examples of "be it until you are it." If you want to become more self-disciplined, if you want to become more confident, or whatever your goal is, act the part. Observe self-disciplined people. Imagine what a confident person would do. However, you want to expand your sense of identity, act like you are that person already.

Seven Master Steps to Lasting Change

Neuro-linguistic programming a science that was developed to understand human behavior and make changes in behavior that empowers the individual. One of the important tools that it uses to produce a change in behavior is referred to as the seven master steps to change (Robbins, 1992). Before getting into the steps, I need to introduce the concept of the six human needs.

The Six Human Needs

Six conditions have been identified that are inherently needed by every human being (Robbins, 1992). The need to fulfill these needs explains all human behavior. The highest level of fulfillment is found when we can meet all six of these needs. The six human needs are Certainty, uncertainty, connection, significance, contribution, and growth.

Certainty: Every person needs a certain level of certainty, meaning that they have some level of control in avoiding painful situations and pursue those that will give them pleasure. Certainty can be as basic as knowing that you can walk across the floor without it collapsing or that your favorite food is waiting for you at home.

All humans need a level of certainty in their life, though each person finds their sense of certainty in their own way. For one person, certainty maybe knowing that they have a job, while for another it could be not throwing anything away (such as in hoarding behavior).

Gaining certainty can be also found at the emotional level. Some people experience certainty by being defensive toward others or avoiding commitment in relationships. By behaving this way, they avoid anybody getting close to them. They gain a sense of certainty that comes from not being vulnerable in relationships.

Uncertainty: Just as we all need a sense of certainty, all of us need a sense of uncertainty. If we were certain about everything, there would be no personal growth, and we would be bored with life. For this reason, we seek excitement and variety in life. That we have a need for uncertainty and certainty is no mistake. A balanced life is one where we find a way to meet both of these needs.

Significance: The third human need is feeling significant. All humans need to feel a sense of significance, that their lives matter. To feel significant requires that we be able to somehow stand out from others.

As humans, we have found innumerable ways to feel significant. A short list of examples would be finding significance through your work, your social standing, in your abilities or talents, in your physical appearance, and through service to others. However, some people find significance through negative means, including exploiting others and committing crimes like mass shootings. As with the opposing needs of certainty and uncertainty, we need to develop a healthy balance of significance and connection.

Connection: The fourth human need is a sense of connection. All of us need to be able to connect to something outside ourselves. We can gain connection through other people, through animals, objects, and through spirituality, how each person finds connection with others can vary. While some people connect to others through friendship or love, some find connection with others through unhealthy ways. Some people find connection in extreme political groups such as hate groups or through cults.

Contribution: The fifth human need is contribution. We all need to be able to contribute to others; we all need to feel that we can make a difference in the world.

Growth: The sixth and final human need is the need for growth. We all need to feel that we are growing as human beings, that our lives are evolving. If we do not grow, our lives become stagnant.

Now that you understand the six human needs, you are ready to learn about the seven major steps to lasting change, a technique that you can use to create any personal change that you want to achieve.

The seven steps are: Understand your view of the world, identify and create leverage, break your pattern, redefine the problem, create empowering alternatives, condition your new behavior, and relate your new behavior to your life's purpose or mission.

Step 1: Understand your worldview

To understand your worldview is to understand why you do the things that you do. No human behavior is carried out without an intention for doing so. The intention behind all of your behaviors, without exception, is to meet one of the six human needs. Ultimately, the reason behind everything that you do is to achieve a feeling of certainty, uncertainty, significance, connection, growth, contribution, or a combination of these.

The only reason why we repeat behavior is that there is a payoff for it. The behavior fulfilled one or more of the six human needs. A person who lacks self-discipline chooses to be this way whether they are conscious of it or not.

Why would someone choose not to demonstrate self-discipline? Perhaps it meets their need for certainty. The person may believe that not initiating a project is less risky to their self-esteem than it is to attempt the project and not succeed. Also, not demonstrating self-discipline may also meet their need for significance. After all, if they are undisciplined, people may pay attention to them by giving me advice. Getting their attention may make them feel significant, not to mention meeting their need for connection.

Identify the behaviors that are preventing you from achieving your life's dreams and determine which of the six human needs is getting met by them.

Step 2: Find and Create Leverage

Once you have identified the human needs that are being met by the behavior that you are trying to change, you need to create leverage by connecting with all the pain that the behavior has cost you in your life. The best way to do this is using one of the techniques that you learned for changing a belief (Chapter 3). What you want to do is to connect with all the painful experiences that engaging in this behavior has caused you in every aspect of your life, including emotionally, physically, socially, economically, and spiritually.

Step 3: Break the Pattern

As mentioned before, all behaviors that we repeat are due to receiving a payoff for them. Since the behavior meets one of the six human needs, the behavior is reinforced. What is needed is to interrupt the pattern of the behavior that you are trying to change.

Create a list of strategies that you can use to interrupt the pattern of your behavior when you find yourself engaging in it. Example: If the behavior I am trying to change is avoiding being self-disciplined, I may remind myself of all the ways that not being self-disciplined has caused me pain in my life. Or, I can think about the best way to handle the task that needs to be done. If you repeatedly interrupt the pattern of the behavior, it will eventually lose its potency.

Step 4: Redefine the Problem

Redefining the problem means looking for the root cause. I may have thought that my problem was a lack of self-discipline. Based on Step 1, I may realize that not demonstrating self-discipline meets my need for certainty. Doing this feels safer than taking on a goal and not succeeding. Instead of seeing as a lack of self-discipline as being the problem, I need to redefine the problem: What can I do to meet my need for certainty that will at the same time allow me to pursue my goals for a happier life.

Step 5: Create an Alternative

When you have identified the root cause of your behavior, when you have identified which of the six human needs your current behavior is meeting, it is time to find a way to meet that need in a positive way. Example: If my lack of self-discipline met my need for certainty, my new empowering way to meet that need will learn goal setting and planning so that I can create a structured pathway toward the goal that I desire.

Step 6: Condition the New Behavior

The current behavior that you are trying to change became a habit through conditioning. Your behavior was reinforced because one or more of your six human needs were met. Because the behavior was reinforced, you repeated the behavior until it became a habit.

In Step 6, you are going to use the same process to reinforce your new behavior. Example: If my new way of gaining certainty is to practice goal setting and planning, I am going to reward myself every time I engage in goal setting or planning. In the beginning, my new behavior will become reinforced by my rewarding myself and having my needs met. Eventually, I will not have to reward myself because the behavior will be rewarding in itself.

Step 7: Relate to my purpose in life.

The final step is to create a connection between the change that you want to achieve and your life purpose. Example: The change that I want to make is to create greater certainty in myself so that I can achieve my life's purpose. If my life purpose is to create happiness for others through my creative skills, I am going to connect the development of my sense of certainty with my ability to share my creativity with others.

Finding your purpose ultimately involves looking within to discover what resonates with you and finding a way to do what you love in a way that meets the needs of others. One of the best ways to look within is through mediation, which is also great for developing self-discipline.

Chapter 7: Level 5 Exercises

Meditating for Self Discipline

One of the most powerful and direct ways to cultivate self-discipline and gain deep insight into yourself is through meditation. Why is meditation a great way to develop self-discipline? There are two reasons for this. The first reason is that it requires a level of self-discipline to practice meditation. The reason for this is that to meditate successfully requires that you let go lifelong patterns you have developed.

For most of us, our focus of attention is on the world around us. We focus on other people, in places, and things. However, there is an inner world, a world that lies within us, which also is a target of our focus. We focus on our thoughts, our perceptions, and our sensations.

When we have a thought, we can become lost in it to the point where we are oblivious to what is happening around us. We may perceive images, such as when dreaming, daydreaming, or during altered states. During this time, we can be transported to another world. Emotions, feelings, and the act of touching an object are collectively referred to as sensations of the body. We often define the kind of day we are having based on the sensations that we experience.

We are so focused on the object of the inner world that we identify with them. They form our sense of who we are, especially with thought.

The only reason why you feel that you have challenges with self-discipline is that you identify with that thought. The power of meditation is that it places you in a position of realizing, through direct experience, that you are not your thoughts, perceptions, or your sensations.

Finally, by committing to meditate each day, you are developing your self-discipline. To further understand the relationship that we have with our mind, here is a short story.

The Servant and the Master

There was a servant who had served his master for many years. Despite all his years of service, the servant never actually saw his master! His master, who lived in a huge estate, never left his bedroom. All these years, the servant simply performed the tasks that were communicated to him by his master, which was always through the closed door of the bedroom.

One day, the servant encountered a problem. He went to his master's room and knocked on the door. When there was no response, the servant knocked a second time. Because the servant still received no response, he became worried.

The servant then noticed his master's door was unlocked, something that he had never seen before. Concerned about his master's welfare, the servant opened the door. What he saw left him in disbelief: the room was empty! There was no furniture, no carpet, no drapes, and no master! The servant had a sudden realization: He had been toiling all these years for a master that did not exist!

In this story, the servant symbolizes you and me. The master represents the mind. Most of us have lived our lives giving our mind blind allegiance. We have personalized certain thoughts and from that have created our sense of identity.

As stated earlier, our sense of identity is nothing more but a set of beliefs that we have of ourselves. These beliefs create the lens through which we experience ourselves and the world around us. What we believe is greatly shaped by how we interpret our experiences in life.

Normally, whenever we pursue something that we desire, we will eventually find ourselves at the crossroads where our sense of doubt intersects the pursuit of our desire. This is the point where everything that we were ever told by our parents, our families, our circle of friends, our education, society, and conventional wisdom comes to roost, informing us of all the reasons why we should give up our pursuit. You may experience thoughts like "You always failed in the past, what makes you think you will succeed this time?" "You are not smart enough," "You are too old to pursue your wild dreams," or "You have responsibilities to take care of. Don't be selfish."

The power of our distracting thoughts is purely illusionary. Thoughts are just like photographs in a photo album. A photograph is just a representation of an object; however, the photograph is not the object itself. The photograph of an old automobile is not the automobile. You cannot drive a photograph. Such is our thoughts.

Our thoughts are the mental representation of our experiences both past and future. Our anticipations or anxieties are the snapshots created by the mind as it contemplates the future, while our memories, regrets, and sentimentalities are the snapshots of the mind as it recalls the past. In either case, they just interpretations of the mind. It is when we unquestionably take these interpretations as being a truth that they become our reality.

Thoughts are inherently powerless, all the power that we perceive them to have over us comes from us projecting our power on to them. The moon does not generate its own light; it is dependent on the sun. It is the sun's light reflecting off the moon that gives its illumination. Our thoughts receive all their power from the attention that we give them.

We experience an innumerable number of thoughts each day; however, the majority of them slip under the radar of our attention. It is when thoughts become the recipient of our attention that we find them significant. We find them significant because we have assigned meaning to them. Within themselves, thoughts and beliefs are both meaningless and powerless.

If you wish to become self-disciplined, you must turn the tables on your mind. You can learn how to take charge of your mind and make it your servant. The following are beginning exercises to guide your awareness inward so that you can develop greater insights into the nature of your inner world. They will also the lay foundation for more advanced meditations that will come later.

Visualization Exercise

1. Sit down and make yourself comfortable and relaxed.

2. When you are feeling relaxed, close your eyes and imagine in your mind a full moon. Make this image as real as you can make it.

3. Now imagine a black cat. Again, try to experience it as vividly as possible.

4. Finally, imagine a red sports car. Make it as real as possible.

5. Now open your eyes.

You just imagined a full moon, a black cat, and a red sports car. These images were a form of thought. Additionally, you most likely did not confuse any of these objects with yourself. Instead, you just observed them.

The reason why you did not identify with these thoughts is that they were most likely meaningless to you. However, there are plenty of other thoughts that you do identify with.

You so strongly identify some of these thoughts that you experience yourself as them. The reason why we identify with some thoughts is that we personalize by making them meaningful to us. We do this by giving them our continuous attention, which leads to some crucial points as to the nature of thought:

- Thoughts have no inherent power or meaning. It is us who give meaning to a thought. Thoughts gain all their power from the attention that we give them.

- Since all thoughts are of the same nature, you can remain as the observer of any thought without being impacted by it. Your most nagging thought can be as innocuous as your thought of the full moon, the black cat, or the sports car.

Exercises for Practicing Nonjudgement

1. Find a place where there are minimal distractions and where you feel comfortable.

2. When you are ready, take your time to look at your surroundings.

3. As you observe your surroundings, rate your experience of observing. How enjoyable was it? How did your body feel? Did it feel heavy or light? Was your mind full of thoughts or was in quiet?

4. Now close your eyes and imagine that you are an alien from outer space. You have landed on this planet to study it. As an alien, you have no prior knowledge of Earth. For this reason, you have no knowledge to rely on, no experience that you can draw upon, and no anticipation of what you will discover. What this means is that when observing this planet there is no room for any form of

judgment or analysis. All that you can do is observe without judgment.

5. Now open your eyes and observe your surroundings.

   What is it like to observe your surroundings without any form of judgment, thoughts of the future, or any references to the past? Did your second observation appear fresher or purer? Check within yourself: How are you feeling? Do you feel more still and calmer?

   If you were successful in this exercise, you would have briefly experienced a greater connection with your environment as well as with yourself. If you had trouble with it (as with all the exercises in this course), continue to practice them until there is a change in how you experience yourself and the world.

Developing Concentration of Awareness

One way to learn self-discipline is to develop your ability to concentrate your awareness. Normally, our attention is fragmented by all the busyness that is occurring within our minds and around us. The following is a straightforward and well-known exercise for developing a greater concentration of awareness by observing the breath. Do the following:

1. Sit down in a comfortable position and close your eyes.

2. Allow yourself to breathe normally for a few minutes. While doing so, notice the sensations of body and breath.

3. When you feel a sense that you are becoming more relaxed and aware of the body, place your attention on your breath.

4. Allow your attention to follow your breath as it enters your body while inhaling. Experience the sensations of your breath as it travels inward.

5. As you exhale, allow your awareness to follow your breath as it courses through your body toward your nostrils or mouth. Feel the sensations as the air leaves your body.

6. During this exercise, your mind is bound to wander as you experience thoughts that compete for your attention. This is both normal and okay, do not judge yourself or your thoughts for this. Simply accept that your attention was distracted and gently return your attention to your breath. Do this as often as necessary.

7. As you do this exercise, notice that your thoughts come and ago. While your thoughts come and go, you do not. You are the one that is aware of thought coming and going. You are the one that is aware of thought, but you are not your thoughts. If your mind becomes calmer, it is because you are not giving thoughts your attention. Whatever you focus on becomes stronger. Whatever you withdraw your attention from grows weaker. To understand

this through direct experience is a key to developing self-discipline.

With repeated practice of this exercise, you will find that your mind will grow calmer, your concentration will become greater, and you will find yourself experiencing greater awareness of the movement of thought. You may wish to make this a daily practice, extending the duration of the exercise as you improve in practice. It is especially useful to practice in the morning before starting your day.

Making the Mind your Servant

The exercises that you previously did in this section provided you with guidance for starting the process of reclaiming your power over the mind. Exercise 1 was intended to demonstrate that your thoughts are not *who you are*. Exercise 2 was intended to demonstrate that your thoughts (which include judgment) distort your experience of reality. Exercise 3 was intended to confirm further that you are not your thoughts. Moreover, your thoughts are powerless if you do not energize them with your attention. By focusing on your breath, you deprived your thoughts of the attention they demand. It is for this reason that you experienced a sense of calmness and stillness.

The following exercises will use the foundation that you built from the previous exercises. Please do not advance to these exercises until you feel comfortable with the previous ones. Also, when doing the exercises in the next section, do not advance to the next exercise until you are comfortable doing the current exercise.

Meditation 1

One of the reasons why many of us do not trust ourselves is because we do not listen to the feelings that we experience in the body. Our feelings are part of the body's energy field, and it acts as an internal guidance system. When we are relaxed, we experience pleasurable sensations. When we perceive fear, we experience feelings in the body that prepare the body to react. Learning to be aware of your feelings, to listen to them, and trust them, is critical to developing self-discipline. If you do not trust your feelings, you will give your trust to someone or something outside of yourself.

1. Close your eyes and allow yourself to follow your breath during inhalation and exhalation. Place your attention on your breath. Feel it as it courses through your body.

2. Now place your attention on the sensations of the body. Place your attention on any sensation of the body that appears in your awareness.

3. Do you feel a tingling in your hands or feet? Do you feel tension in your back, shoulders, or face? Do you feel the weight of your body or the pressure on your buttocks from the chair or ground that you are sitting on?

4. Allow yourself to experience the sensations of the body without any judgment of any of them, even the ones that may feel unpleasant. Sensations are just that sensations, there are no good or bad sensations. Good and bad, pleasant and unpleasant, these are value judgments that exist solely in mind. The same thing is true with perceptions, sounds, and thoughts; they just exist.

5. Are the sensations that you experience stable? Are they always the same or do they change? Are they always there or do they come and go?

   Just as with thoughts, your feelings are in constant flux. No thought or feeling is permanent. What is constant is the awareness that knows of thoughts and feelings. Your awareness is never in flux. You are the source of awareness.

Meditation on Feelings

What prevents most of us from experiencing a true sense of our power and inner peace is our tendencies to resist, deny, or suppress those emotions and feelings that we find unpleasant. When we do so, we are turning our backs to what is equivalent to our GPS Navigating System.

Our emotions and feelings are like a compass that informs us of the nature of our thoughts and decision making; they indicate whether what we are thinking or doing is aligned with our highest good.

When we can allow ourselves to fully experience our emotions and feelings, we can learn to trust ourselves.

Meditation 2

In this first meditation, you will learn to bring greater awareness to your emotions and feelings.

1. Sit down in a comfortable position and close your eyes.

2. Allow yourself to follow your breath during inhalation and exhalation. Place your attention on your breath. Feel it as it courses through your body.

3. Take on an attitude of complete allowing, that whatever arises in this meditation that you have complete acceptance of it.

4. Observe the perceptions, thoughts, sensations, feelings, and emotions that arise within you. Allow them to come and go on their own accord. All you need to do is be the observer of them.

5. Now pay attention to any emotion that arises. Become an observer of it, what happens when your focus is placed on your emotion?

6. Do not place any meaning on the emotion or feelings that you experience; do not think of them as being positive or negative. Words such as "positive," "negative," "pleasant," or "unpleasant" are products of the mind

7. There is no intrinsic meaning to anything in life. All meaning is derived from our minds. Emotions and feelings have no power

of their own; they derive all their power from the attention we give them.

8. When observing emotions or feelings, do so with complete allowing, do not try to change anything about them.

9. As you observe your emotions and feelings, do you notice a change in how you experience them? Do they change in intensity? Do they become stronger or milder? Can you locate where the emotions come from? Can you observe where they go?

10. As you observe emotions, ask yourself "Am I my emotions and feelings or am I the one that is aware of them?" If a feeling or emotion or feeling is experienced as being unpleasant, does awareness that is observing them feel unpleasant? If an emotion or feeling is experienced as being pleasant, does the awareness that is observing them feel pleasant?

11. Awareness does not experience anything; awareness can only know of experience. Awareness is like a beam of light shining on a snow-covered field. The light does not feel the cold of the snow; it only illuminates it. As you observe emotions, be as the beam of light.

Meditation on Thought

This next exercise provides the opportunity to gain greater awareness of the nature of thought. Note: This exercise is lengthier than the previous exercises. Because of this, it is recommended that you familiarize yourself with the exercise before doing it. You may also consider recording this exercise on a voice recorder and replay it when you do the exercise. As previously stated, it is recommended that you practice any of the exercises before advancing to the next section.

Do the following:

1. Find a comfortable place that is relatively free from distractions.

2. Sit down and allow yourself to relax.

3. Close your eyes and place your attention on your breath. Be aware of the sensations of your breath as it enters into your body, fills your chest, and as it is released from your body during exhalation.

4. Maintain your focus on the movement and sensations of your breath.

5. Inevitably, thoughts will appear. When thoughts do appear, return your attention to your breath. Do not provide any attention to the thoughts that appear. To do this means that you are not to react, evaluate, judge, or analyze any thoughts. Your only job is to acknowledge that they have appeared in your awareness and then return your focus to your breath.

6. As you become more practiced at this exercise, you will notice an increase in calmness and stillness as the activity of your thoughts diminish. When you experience this state, do the following:

Focus your attention on a thought as you become aware of its presence. Observe your thoughts without getting involved with its content. Do not try to resist, change, or judge any of your thoughts. Treat your thought as though it is a rare bird which you are just observing and studying.

7. As you learn to observe your thoughts, you will notice some of their interesting qualities. Here are a few questions that you can ask yourself:

    a. Where do my thoughts arise from?

    b. Do my thoughts change or are they fixed? Do they change in their intensity?

    c. Where do my thoughts go when they fade away?

    It is important to note at this point that these questions are not intellectual questions. Instead, become curious and attempt to answer them purely through your actual observation. Further, finding answers to these questions is less important than the actual inquiry.

8. Now observe a thought until it fades away from your awareness. Before the next thought appears, what do you see? What do you experience?

    This last exercise may take practice before you become skillful enough to develop the level of awareness where you can respond to these questions. If you are serious about developing a disciplined mind, this exercise is worth it!

Chapter 8: Procrastination

Hopefully, you will use the information that you have learned from this book to start cultivating self-discipline and purse the goals that you have for your life. If you ever tried to develop self-discipline before but gave up, or if you never actually put in the effort to expand your self-discipline, you gave in to the twin forces of pain and pleasure.

It was mentioned earlier that all human behavior is governed by the two forces of pain and pleasure. We are wired to avoid painful experiences and move toward pleasurable one. It was also stated that whether an experience is painful or pleasurable is based on our interpretation of it. What may be unpleasant for some people may be desirable to others. Most people fear or dislike snakes, while others are fascinated with snakes and keep them as pets.

Procrastination occurs when we perceive doing a task as being more painful than it would be if we did not do it. We procrastinate because we associate unpleasant feelings toward performing the task and more favorable feelings toward not doing the task. The balance sheet method will allow you to switch your associations so that you learn to associate unpleasant feelings for putting off the task and pleasant feelings for doing it.

To break through procrastination, consider using the Belief Balance sheet (Robbins, 1992). Here is an example:

1. Identify the reason why you are procrastinating. What is it you are fearful of or trying to avoid? Identify the belief that you have that causing your procrastination.
2. Take a sheet and fold it in half lengthwise.
3. On the top of the paper, write down the limiting beliefs that you identified.
4. After writing down your belief, make a list on the left-hand side of the paper of all the ways that holding this belief has cost you in your life. When writing, keep in mind the following:
   a. When writing this list, write down the first thing that comes to your mind, even if it seems irrelevant.
   b. Write as fast as you can and feel the emotions that arise. This is a heartfelt exercise, not a cerebral one.
   c. Keep writing until you cannot think of what to write.
5. By each item, you write down, assign an arbitrary point value as to how much weight this item has had on you. When selecting the point value, choose the first number that comes to mind.

6. When you have completed assigning the point values, find the total of all the point values and place it at the bottom of the page.
7. For the right side of the page, repeat Steps 3-6, except this time you will write down all the ways that this belief has benefited you.
8. Come up with a new alternative belief, which supports you.
9. On the second paper, repeat steps 2-7, though this time you will do the Steps 4 and 7 in reverse. In other words, write down all the ways that you would believe that you would benefit from this new belief when doing Step 4 and write down all the ways your new belief would cost you in Step 7.
10. When you have completed the two sheets, do the following:
11. Immediately review your lists, allowing yourself to fully experience any emotions that arise.
12. Review your lists every day, once in the morning and once before you go to bed until you become fully associated with the emotions that you experience.

By becoming fully with associated the feelings that you experience when you think of the costs of your old beliefs and the benefits that you would obtain from adopting your new ones, your mind will become reprogrammed with your new belief (Robbins, 1992).

When addressing the issue of procrastination, also consider the following:

- Use the Seven Master Steps to identify which of the six human needs that your procrastination is meeting and find a new empowering alternative.
- Break up the task into small steps and take daily action until you complete it.
- Create a more empowering environment to motivate you to do the task by doing things like playing your favorite music so that performing the task is more enjoyable.

Chapter 9: The Seven Day Plan

In this book, you were given a large amount of information to work with. It is for this reason that this chapter was written. This chapter will give a roadmap for the next seven days on how to use the information that you gained to plot your course to developing self-discipline.

Day 1: Identify the goals that you want to accomplish by doing the Goal Setting exercise from Chapter 3.

Days 2-3: Develop a plan for your top 1 year goals. Refer to the section Planning for suggestions. You may not be able to plan all the steps involved that are required to achieve your goal but do identify the steps that you are available.

Day 4: Identify your limiting beliefs that may cause you problems as you pursue your goals. Do the Belief Balance Sheet exercise so that you can start the process of changing that belief.

Day 5: Identify your values by doing the Value System exercise. Identify your values and come up with empowering ways for you to experience them while being in full control of the process.

Day 6: From Chapter 4, do the exercises on contribution. By doing these exercises, you will start the process of discovering how you can use your passions to serve others while developing self-discipline.

Day 7: Based on the previous exercises, determine the one thing that you want to change about yourself that would allow you to move forward to reaching your desired goals. Use the exercises in the section "Be it until you do it" to start the process of becoming the person that you want to be.

All the other exercises can be used to reinforce, refine, or expand your understandings of what you experienced in the first week. Use the exercises that resonate with you and use them as you feel is needed.

What happens after the first seven days? I want you to use whatever you gained in the first week and focus on developing it further. If you gain a greater understanding of your limited beliefs, I want you to put more energy into reinforcing your new empowering belief.

If you gained greater clarity in your values, I want you to expand upon that by developing ways to experience your values in a way where you are in full control of the process. I do not want you to develop the ways of experiencing them; I want you to use them. If you gained a greater understanding of what drives you, put your passions into action and contribute to others.

Every exercise in this book is designed to bring you closer to developing self-discipline as well as further empowering you to achieve the goals that you desire. Becoming an expert in any one of these exercises will move you in the direction that you want. Think of the exercises as a buffet. Serve yourself by using the exercises that seem right for you and stick with it until you succeed in getting what you want!

Conclusion

Imagine a lantern whose light illuminates the surrounding area. Now imagine a laser beam whose narrow beam of light focuses on a specific spot. When our attention is not disciplined, we are like the lantern. When we are behaving in a self-disciplined way, our attention is like the laser beam. It is focused on that which will benefit us, and those we care about, in the long term.

Learning to become self-disciplined is learning how to focus our attention. All of us can focus our attention if we encounter something that is meaningful to us. Even a child with attention deficit order will be able to focus their attention on a toy or game that they love.

The purpose of this book was to give you the tools to strengthen your attention and discover what that which is meaningful to you, be it your goals, your life's purpose, or transforming your identity. You have always been, and always will be the source of attention. My hope is that you will use this book to learn how to illuminate the world around you with your light while achieving your dreams with laser focus.

References

American Psychological Association. (n.d). *What You Need to Know about Willpower: The Psychological Science of Self-Control.*

American Psychological Association. n.d. *Strengthening Self-Control*

Association for Psychological Services (2012).*Where Does Self-Discipline Come From?*

Dickler, Jessica (2017*). Most Americans live paycheck to paycheck. CNBC.*

Gregoire, Carolyn (2013). Happiness Index: Only 1 In 3 Americans Are Very Happy, According To Harris Poll. *Huffington Post.*

Mason, Kyla.C, (2014). *Percentage of Americans with college degrees rises, paying for degrees tops financial challenges.* PBS.

Murry, Christopher; Ng, Marie; and Mokdad, Ali (2014). *The vast majority of American adults are overweight or obese, and weight is a growing problem among US children.* IHME

Robbins, Tony (1992). *Awaken the Giant Within.* Simon and Schuster. ISBN: 0671791540

Tian, A. D., Schroeder, J., Häubl, G., Risen, J. L., Norton, M. I., & Gino, F. (2018). Enacting rituals to improve self-control. *Journal of Personality and Social Psychology.*

Disclaimer

The information contained in **"Self-Discipline Science & Daily Self-Discipline -2 In 1-"** and its components, is meant to serve as a comprehensive collection of strategies that the author of this eBook has done research about. Summaries, strategies, tips and tricks are only recommendations by the author, and reading this eBook will not guarantee that one's results will exactly mirror the author's results.

The author of this Ebook has made all reasonable efforts to provide current and accurate information for the readers of this eBook. The author and its associates will not be held liable for any unintentional errors or omissions that may be found.

The material in the Ebook may include information by third parties. Third party materials comprise of opinions expressed by their owners. As such, the author of this eBook does not assume responsibility or liability for any third party material or opinions.

The publication of third party material does not constitute the author's guarantee of any information, products, services, or opinions contained within third party material. Use of third party material does not guarantee that your results will mirror our results. Publication of such third party material is simply an recommendation and expression of the author's own opinion of that material.

Whether because of the progression of the Internet, or the unforeseen changes in company policy and editorial submission guidelines, what is stated as fact at the time of this writing may become outdated or inapplicable later.